More Praise for *The Self-Made Myth*

"Miller and Lapham have powerfully demonstrated that there is no self-made man or woman. Individual success is absolutely dependent on public contributions to infrastructure, education, health, transportation, the stock market, and other protections of all kinds. If you use a computer, you are using the public's research contributions to satellites, GPS systems, the Internet, and decades of computer science funding. Self-made? Ridiculous."

—**George Lakoff, author of** *The Political Mind* **and** *Don't Think of an Elephant!*

"Whether it was my father getting educated on the GI bill or the guy at the Small Business Administration encouraging me, I have always counted my blessings and been aware of my responsibility to give back. *The Self-Made Myth* reminds us that we should be grateful for all government does to support individual and business success in this country."

—**Wayne Silby, Founding Chair, Calvert Funds**

"Small business owners are often put forward as the poster children for antiregulatory, antigovernment, and antitax measures that we don't support and that are frankly eroding the infrastructure that has made this country so great. This powerful and well-written book couldn't come at a better time. I urge anyone who cares about public policy to read *The Self-Made Myth* and share it widely."

—**Katharine D. Myers, co-owner, Myers-Briggs Type Indicator**

"*The Self-Made Myth* could be a political game changer. Powerful, compelling, and well researched, it gives serious meaning to the term *community wealth* and demolishes what may be the most destructive myth in America. I urge everyone to read it, absorb it, promote it, and share it with friends and relatives."

—**David Korten, Board Chair,** *YES! Magazine,* **and author of** *Agenda for a New Economy* **and** *When Corporations Rule the World*

"At this critical time in our country's history, *The Self-Made Myth*'s message about the vitally important role of government in the success of individuals, businesses, and the nation is a must-read. Miller and Lapham expose the dangerous and self-serving course espoused by those interested only in furthering their political, personal, or corporate success while pulling up the ladder of opportunity for others."
—**Frank Knapp, Jr., Vice Chair, American Sustainable Business Council, and President and CEO, South Carolina Small Business Chamber of Commerce**

"We take for granted the interdependence of successful for-profit ventures and a civil society (laws, taxes, and a shared responsibility for the commons). *The Self-Made Myth* is an elegant statement of the case and an excellent reminder to put forward the argument or forfeit the future."
—**Trish Karter, cofounder, Dancing Deer Baking Company**

"*The Self-Made Myth* rebuts the idea that the wealthy got rich entirely through their hard work and talent. The public must recognize that none of us can succeed on our own. The wealth the country as a whole enjoys is the result of the physical and social infrastructure we have collectively created; unfortunately, the rules have been rigged so that a small minority gets to enjoy the bulk of the benefits. As Miller and Lapham compellingly argue, this must change."
—**Dean Baker, economist, writer, and Codirector, Center for Economic and Policy Research**

"*The Self-Made Myth* will change the way we think about taxes and policy as we enter a great debate on the role of public investment in the success of business. We have a profound responsibility to our children and grandchildren to invent ways to make sure the new American Dream is an economy with heart. This book is an important tool for getting us there."
—**Jeffrey Hollender, founder, Jeffrey Hollender Partners, and cofounder, Seventh Generation**

The
Self-Made
Myth

The
Self-Made
Myth

And the Truth about How Government Helps
Individuals and Businesses Succeed

361.05
miller

Brian Miller

and

Mike Lapham

BK

Berrett–Koehler Publishers, Inc.
San Francisco
a BK Currents book

Berrett-Koehler Publishers, Inc.
235 Montgomery Street, Suite 650, San Francisco, CA 94104-2916
Tel: (415) 288-0260   Fax: (415) 362-2512   www.bkconnection.com

Ordering Information

Quantity sales. Special discounts are available on quantity purchases by corporations, associations, and others. For details, contact the "Special Sales Department" at the Berrett-Koehler address above.

Individual sales. Berrett-Koehler publications are available through most bookstores. They can also be ordered directly from Berrett-Koehler:
Tel: (800) 929-2929; Fax: (802) 864-7626; www.bkconnection.com.

Orders for college textbook/course adoption use. Please contact Berrett-Koehler: Tel: (800) 929-2929; Fax: (802) 864-7626.

Orders by U.S. trade bookstores and wholesalers. Please contact Ingram Publisher Services, Tel: (800) 509-4887; Fax: (800) 838-1149; E-mail: customer.service@ ingrampublisherservices.com; or visit www.ingrampublisherservices.com/Ordering for details about electronic ordering.

Berrett-Koehler and the BK logo are registered trademarks of Berrett-Koehler Publishers, Inc.

Printed in the United States of America

Berrett-Koehler books are printed on long-lasting acid-free paper. When it is available, we choose paper that has been manufactured by environmentally responsible processes. These may include using trees grown in sustainable forests, incorporating recycled paper, minimizing chlorine in bleaching, or recycling the energy produced at the paper mill.

Library of Congress Cataloging-in-Publication Data
Miller, Brian, 1968–
    The self-made myth : and the truth about how government helps individuals and businesses succeed / Brian Miller and Mike Lapham.
        p. cm.
    Includes bibliographical references and index.
    ISBN 978-1-60994-506-0 (pbk.)
1. Economic assistance, Domestic—United States. 2. Subsidies—United States.
3. Social mobility—United States. I. Lapham, Mike. II. Title.
    HC110.P63M53 2012
    361'.05—dc23
                                                          2011048743

17   16   15   14   13   12   10   9   8   7   6   5   4   3   2   1

Cover design by Ian Shimkoviak/The Book Designers.
Interior design and composition by Gary Palmatier, Ideas to Images.
Elizabeth von Radics, copyeditor; Mike Mollett, proofreader; Medea Minnich, indexer.

*For Julian and Ani—may we leave the
world in a better place for you*

BRIAN MILLER

*For my parents and for the members of
Responsible Wealth, who recognize that their
good fortune is not all their own doing*

MIKE LAPHAM

Contents

CHAPTER 5

Policy Implications and the
Public Investment Imperative　　　　130

CONCLUSION

A Call to Action　　　　　　151

Foreword by Bill Gates Sr.

Brian Miller and Mike Lapham have very effectively debunked the pervasive self-made myth that lies at the core of our public policy debates today. When pundits or candidates describe progressive taxes as "punishing success," the implication is that success is achieved by the entrepreneur alone, with little or no help from others. I don't subscribe to that view.

Miller and Lapham provide an important new narrative—one that accounts for the immense role that government plays in business success. Anyone interested in public policy, and particularly tax policy—including our politicians in Washington, DC, and statehouses across the country—should read this book and reflect on its message.

The reader will be edified by the book's thorough examination of the ways that government investment supports business success. To choose just one example, publicly funded research from government agencies like the National Institutes of Health has produced economically and medically valuable products that financially benefit both the research institution itself and the entrepreneurs who develop those products. You may agree with me that this public investment also delivers an enormous benefit for all of us.

As an attorney for almost 50 years, I worked closely with entrepreneurs and saw how their business enterprises are boosted by government efforts to create a stable and positive business environment. I also had a front-row seat for the creation and the growth of my son's business (Microsoft), and I observed the many ways our country's publicly supported infrastructure, tax laws, government-funded research, education, patent protection, and so forth helped the company grow. As I've said numerous times, I have no doubt that growing the company in the fertile soil of the United States accounts for a significant portion of the value of that enterprise; and if you had plunked Bill down in some developing country, even with all of his intelligence, creativity, and hard work, the company would probably have gone nowhere. Being born in this country is the ingredient that most reliably determines whether a person has the *opportunity* to become wealthy.

The Self-Made Myth recapitulates and reinforces the government's role in supporting business and makes the case for progressive taxation and a robust public sector. With a deeper understanding of the roots of individual and business success, one can no longer see progressive taxes as "punishing success" but rather as giving back to support the nation that made one's wealth possible and laying the foundation for the next generation of entrepreneurs.

Some readers may be aware that I have spent a good bit of my time since 2001 advocating for a strong estate tax. I also co-chaired the effort to enact the first-ever income tax in Washington State in 2009. It's critical that we rethink our tax structure in this country, and Miller and Lapham take an important step in that direction by upending the self-made myth and the anti-government narrative that flows from it.

A quick glance at the past 80 years shows that we have had periods of tremendous economic growth in this country when top marginal tax rates were high, putting a lie to the notion that raising taxes on upper-income taxpayers will stunt growth.

At a time when our country is cutting and canceling all sorts of the most basic relief for our disadvantaged citizens, there is a need for our wealthy class to pay income tax in a sum commensurate with the major contribution our society has provided for them. The work of the authors here has made so very clear the need in this difficult era to provide a level of public support that invests in the future of our country.

It is critical to change the conversation about how wealth is created, who creates it, and the role of government, and this book does that effectively and importantly. And it couldn't be timelier. I urge you to read this book and get engaged in the debate about progressive taxes.

Bill Gates Sr. worked for many years as a successful attorney in Seattle, Washington, and is active in philanthropy. He has been an active leader in both the national and Washington State debates around progressive tax policies.

Foreword by Chuck Collins

The debate over taxing the wealthy inevitably gets bogged down in two competing worldviews or narrative stories about wealth and deservedness in the United States. *The Self-Made Myth* goes to the heart of that debate. On the one hand, some argue that we should not tax the wealthy because these individuals earned their wealth alone and, as such, government has no right to tax it.

But there is another view put forth in this book that begins with an understanding that no individual is an island. No one starts a business or creates wealth in a social vacuum. There are things we do together—through our tax dollars and public expenditures— that create the fertile ground for wealth creation. Without these social investments—education, scientific research, and infrastructure—there would be significantly less private wealth.

In 2004 I co-authored a report from United for a Fair Economy, titled "I Didn't Do It Alone: Society's Contribution to Individual Wealth and Success," that examined the multiple factors that contribute to individual success. In *The Self-Made Myth*, Miller and Lapham have elevated that effort to an entirely new level.

One great feature of *The Self-Made Myth* is the personal stories from successful business leaders who describe the web of societal supports that make their private wealth possible. In their stories they talk of schools, libraries, public transportation, scholarships, research—and larger public institutions that protect property rights, build and maintain infrastructure, and facilitate a stable marketplace.

As a result, their attitudes about taxation are refreshingly different. They view taxes as the price we pay to live in a healthy society—with adequate services, infrastructure, and equal opportunity. They understand that for future generations to have the same opportunities that they had, we each have to pay forward to ensure that the ground remains healthy and productive.

Instead of feeling resentful, these fortunate individuals feel gratitude to live in a society with such opportunities. Having received the gift, they want to pass it on. The voices of these wealthy individuals and business leaders are critical to the public policy debates of today. In this new narrative and these powerful examples lies the possibility for a positive future.

Chuck Collins is a senior scholar at the Institute for Policy Studies and the co-editor of www.inequality.org. He is co-author, with Bill Gates Sr., of Wealth and Our Commonwealth: Why America Should Tax Accumulated Fortunes. *In 1995 he co-founded United for a Fair Economy.*

Preface

This book is born of nearly 15 years of organizing and working with business leaders and other high-income and high-wealth individuals as part of the Responsible Wealth project. Responsible Wealth is a network of 700 business leaders and high-wealth individuals who speak out in favor of progressive tax policies, corporate accountability, and fair wages. They do so because they have a deeper and more honest understanding of their own wealth and financial success, an understanding we call the *built-together reality*, which we lift up in this book.

Responsible Wealth is a project of United for a Fair Economy (UFE), a national organization working across class lines to raise awareness of the dangers of extreme inequality and to promote a more broadly shared prosperity. The authors of this book, Brian Miller and Mike Lapham, are the executive director of UFE and the project director of Responsible Wealth, respectively. For additional information about Miller, Lapham, UFE, and Responsible Wealth, see "About the Authors" at the back of this book.

When doing radio and TV interviews and speaking around the nation, we have seen debates about tax policy and other issues break down over different views of what's fair and what can be morally justified. We argue in this book that those differing views of fairness are rooted in starkly differing understandings of the origins of wealth and financial success. So instead of arguing about policies, this book is devoted to reaching a deeper understanding of the origins of individual and business success. Is wealth creation and business success the result of the hard work, creativity, and sacrifice of a small number of self-made men and women? Or is wealth the result of a broad array of actors and forces, hard work being only one of them?

The book is organized as follows:

- The introduction offers an overview of the self-made myth and its consequences, as well as a preview of the built-together reality and the paradigm shift it brings about in the way we view the public policy questions of our day.

- Chapter 1 examines the roots of the self-made myth, its more recent adaptations and examples, as well as additional implications of that myth on the debates of our times.

- Chapter 2 makes visible the often-invisible contributions that government and society have made to the success of prominent business leaders. In doing so it busts the myth of self-made wealth and clears the way for a new understanding of success.

- Chapter 3 lays the foundation of the built-together reality of individual and business success, including an examination of the myriad factors that contribute to the success of individuals and businesses.

- Chapter 4 comprises the bulk of the book, featuring profiles based on interviews with business leaders whose first-person accounts paint a very different and more holistic picture of wealth creation—the built-together reality. Chapters 2 and 4 are supplemented with informational "reality checks" that offer historical perspective and analysis of particular ways that government investment supports individual and business success.

- Chapter 5 provides an examination of how the built-together reality dramatically changes the way we view the role of government and points to a number of public policy choices that flow from this new view, from taxes to workers' rights.

■ The conclusion presents a number of ways that readers can get involved in their own communities and social circles to help change the dialogue about individual and business success and foster a more honest debate about the important policy choices we face.

The self-made myth is a story that is told and retold at every level of society and infused into our language and thinking. As such we've written this book with the broad public in mind because we believe that all Americans must engage in this dialogue. We thank you for joining us in this conversation and invite you to share this book far and wide with book clubs, colleagues, friends, and family, including that uncle you always argue about taxes with at holidays, your high school classmate who doesn't understand your politics, and the woman who owns the local shop who's always complaining about taxes and government.

Public Policy and the Success Narrative

Our nation has a deep and proud history of coming together in the face of adversity and challenge. When the Soviets launched *Sputnik 1*—the first manmade satellite to orbit the earth—on October 4, 1957, a challenge had been made. Americans rallied in response, retooling our economy in dramatic ways. Public dollars were put into research and development for new aerospace technologies. Education programs across the nation were ramped up with a new focus on science and math. The space race was on. Many astronauts put their lives on the line, and some lives were lost. But on July 20, 1969, the *Apollo* lander successfully touched down, and the first humans set foot on the moon.

This story represents one of many such moments in our history when Americans came together and solved a problem. In the days following World War II, Americans mobilized to help returning veterans rejoin the economy. Massive public investments in individual opportunity resulted in the GI Bill that enabled those veterans to attend college and buy a home, helping sow the seeds of an unprecedented period of economic prosperity and the rapid expansion of the middle class.

Today we find ourselves facing the lingering effects of the Great Recession. Unemployment is still near double-digit levels. Homes are still being foreclosed upon in record numbers. Banks are still not lending. Despite the enormous challenges we face, our nation seems unable or unwilling to come together and solve the serious problems before us. Instead we are caught in an intractable battle between two opposing views for solving the economic crisis we are in, each arguing that their policy solution is more fair, morally justified, and, in the end, more effective.

We believe that a large part of why we have such differing views in the realm of economic policy is because we have such divergent views on where individual success and wealth come from. In this book we explore a deeply held belief in our society—the myth of the "self-made man," or what we are calling the *self-made myth*—and we offer an alternative that we believe is more honest and complete: the *built-together reality*. These conflicting paradigms are summarized in the table on the following pages (see "At a Glance: The Myth versus the Reality"). It is our hope that by coming to a deeper understanding of the origins of individual wealth and success, we can begin to achieve greater agreement on solutions to the economic crisis we are in and point the way toward a new era of broadly shared prosperity.

The Self-Made Myth

The *self-made myth* is the assertion that individual and business success is the result of the personal characteristics of exceptional individuals, such as hard work, creativity, and sacrifice, with little or no outside assistance. Those who subscribe to this myth do so only by ignoring the contributions of society, the supports made possible through governmental action, any head start a person may have received, and just plain old luck. If this were purely a matter of ego and self-delusion, it would not warrant such a book, but the perpetuation of the self-made myth has profound and destructive impacts on our views of government and the public policy debates of our times.

While its influence has ebbed and flowed over time, the myth of the self-made man has deep roots in our society, dating back to America's earliest history. In a frontier nation with abundant resources, it was argued, any man (women and people of color were largely excluded in those early years) could, through industry and sound character, achieve financial success. Horatio Alger's novels told and retold stories of the poor country boy who made good, while waves of writers touted the accomplishments of nineteenth-century industrialists and entrepreneurs who seemingly rose from rags to riches as testament to this "truth." There were early skeptics who raised legitimate questions, but the story stuck and remains deeply embedded in our national character.

In the mid–twentieth century, writer Ayn Rand brought the self-made man story to new extremes with a book that is nearly required reading for conservative activists today. In Rand's 1957 novel *Atlas Shrugged,* great men are responsible not only for their own success and wealth but for the success and the wealth of the entire world around them. Like the Greek Titan Atlas, they hold the world up on their shoulders. In this fictional world depicted by Rand, the great minds and the self-made titans of industry create virtually all wealth and prosperity in our society. Government only gets in the way.

The tension between society's contributions and those of the individual are evident in our dialogues today. In a nationally tele-vised interview, one of the authors of this book cited a *USA Today* op-ed by Abigail Disney, where she spoke of the role that pub-lic investments—including roads, courts, and schools—played in making her family's fortune possible. The other guest on the show nearly exploded, "It wasn't government! It was *one man!* . . . an entrepreneur named Walt Disney!"[1] This statement overlooks not only society's contributions but also the contributions of Walt's brother and business partner, Roy Disney, grandfather of Abigail. The tendency of our culture to attribute financial success solely to the actions of a single individual is a reflection of the self-made myth in the United States.

At a Glance: The Myth versus the Reality

The Self-Made Myth

The **self-made myth** is the false assertion that individual and business success is entirely the result of the hard work, creativity, and sacrifice of one individual with little outside assistance.

The Anti-government Narrative

The self-made myth is used to justify an **anti-government narrative**.

If all wealth derives from the hard work and the sacrifices of these self-made men and women, there is no significant role for government. Government, if anything, gets in the way in this extreme view.

Furthermore our nation owes a debt of gratitude to these heroes whose business success creates jobs for others and prosperity for all. Those who have not achieved success are simply lazy or risk-averse, according to this worldview.

Implications of the Narrative

If one accepts the self-made myth and the anti-government narrative that flows from it, it follows that:

- Inequalities of wealth and income are justified as a reflection of respective work efforts. Government should do nothing to intervene.

- Progressive taxes are viewed as "punishing success."

- The size of government should be as small as possible, and regulations should be reduced or eliminated to free up the "job creators" to do more of what they do best.

- Efforts to secure fair wages are characterized as extortion from the captains of industry and finance, who supposedly created the wealth.

- Social safety nets are viewed as promoting laziness and sloth.

At a Glance: The Myth Versus the Reality *(continued)*

The Built-Together Reality

The **built-together reality** is the truth that individual and business success is built through individual effort but also through schools, roads, laws, and countless other taxpayer-supported institutions as well as luck, various head starts in life, and the contributions of others.

The Public Investment Imperative

By acknowledging the various factors that contribute to wealth creation, the built-together reality points directly to the **public investment imperative**.

By this view government plays an important role in laying the foundation of individual and business success by investing in schools and transportation, sowing the seeds of innovation, and establishing reliable rules of the road.

The further acknowledgment of luck, various head starts, and the contributions of others erodes the justification for extreme concentrations of wealth and inequality.

Implications of the Narrative

If one accepts the built-together reality and the public investment imperative that flows from it, it follows that:

- Current inequalities of wealth cannot be justified by differing effort alone and should be reduced.

- Progressive taxes are viewed as "giving back" to support the nation that made that wealth possible.

- We need a robust government with the capacity to create the needed regulatory environment and make investments in our shared prosperity.

- Workers who help build the wealth should share in the prosperity through fair wages and a share of the wealth.

- Social safety nets provide an important floor and a much-needed leg up to enable more Americans to join in the building process.

Throughout this book we often use individual and business success interchangeably because what we are talking about is that unique intersection of the individual and the business in which that individual is operating—the entrepreneur, owner, or chief executive officer (CEO)—that is, the "great man" held up by society as the primary driver behind that business's success. It's hard to think of Wal-Mart's rise to market dominance without talking about its founder and long-time CEO, Sam Walton, or to talk about the success of Microsoft without any mention of Bill Gates. The same goes for Steve Jobs and Apple, Lee Iacocca and Chrysler, Phil Knight and Nike, Jack Welch and General Electric, and Mark Zuckerberg and Facebook.

Over the past three or four decades, we've seen a resurgence of the self-made myth, which has been used to fuel an anti-government narrative. It has been used as a political tool to dismantle the social contract that once bound us together as citizens of one nation whose prosperity was interconnected. As far back as Barry Goldwater's *The Conscience of a Conservative* in 1960, we've heard the term "punishing success" applied to progressive tax policies,[2] an assertion that the success of those at the top was entirely their own doing, with no outside help. But that was only the beginning of a much longer assault on government.

We heard lots of talk about "job creators" and "punishing success" during the debate over the Bush tax cuts in 2001 and 2003. We heard it again in late 2009 during the standoff that led to the Obama-GOP tax deal that extended the Bush tax cuts for another two years. And we're hearing it once again as the 2012 presidential race heats up. At a campaign event in Charleston, South Carolina, Texas Governor Rick Perry declared, "As Americans we realize that there is no taxpayer money that wasn't first earned by the sweat and toil of one of our citizens." In this view government and society had no role in the creation of that wealth. It is entirely the result of the "sweat and toil" of individuals acting alone. Perry went on to say that progressive taxation "punishes success."[3]

Mitt Romney echoed this sentiment when he stated, "There was a time in this country where we didn't celebrate attacking people based on their success. We didn't go after people because they were successful."[4] Again, the assertion here is that it was their success and their success alone. Regardless of who emerges as the front-runner in 2012 or who wins the general election, the influence of the self-made myth in our political dialogues will likely continue for years to come.

Of course those who hold the Ayn Rand view take this elevation of the individual to the next level, by not only attributing the success of the *business* to that one individual at the top but attributing the success of the *entire economy* to those self-made individuals. Our public debates today are full of phrases like "job creators," a reference to these mythical heroes whose hard work, creativity, and sacrifice drive our national economy. All public policy must bend to satisfy their perceived needs and wishes. By this view our society would be well served to avoid taking any action that might upset the "job creators."

Implications of the Self-Made Myth and the Anti-government Narrative It Supports

In writing this book, we do not discount the fact that a person, through hard work, creativity, and short-term sacrifice, can better his or her position in life. In most cases one can. To assert that success is *entirely* the result of such individual character traits, with little or no help from others or society, however, has a corrupting impact on our policy debates. How we view the creation of wealth and individual success has a profound influence on our choices of policies to embrace. It shapes our views on taxes, regulations, public investments in schools and vital infrastructure, the legitimacy of extravagant CEO pay, and more.

If one truly believes that wealth derives entirely from the efforts of self-made men, who work harder and take more risks than the rest of us, then extreme inequalities of income and wealth are morally justified as the rewards for that differing work effort. Government should do nothing to intervene. If the successful individuals at the top of our economy are solely responsible for their own fortunes, then they owe nothing back to society, and any effort to tax concentrated wealth and income is akin to "punishing success." The fact that we face the highest levels of inequality the nation has seen since 1928[5] is irrelevant, or perhaps even something to be celebrated, for those who accept this frame.

Furthermore, elevating these individuals to the status of heroic "job creators" encourages us as a nation to cut their taxes even further, despite the adverse impacts that may have on funding available for vital public services. Of course, if wealth is derived entirely from these self-made individuals, then there is little or no role for government. Government should be kept as small as possible by this frame. There is a consistent *anti-government narrative* here, driven in large part by the idea that wealth is entirely the creation of exceptional individuals, with no help from the government.

Finally, by viewing wealth creation and financial success as entirely the result of internal characteristics, those who lack financial security, even if gainfully employed and hardworking, are responsible for their own financial misfortune. Social safety nets are viewed as promoting laziness and sloth. Organizing efforts to secure fair wages are viewed as "thuggery" or as group muggings of the captains of industry and finance who created the wealth.

The Built-Together Reality

We believe the time has come to re-examine how businesses succeed and individual wealth is created. In doing so we develop a more complete picture, one that includes the important role of hard work but also takes into account the role of others and the many roles of government in laying the foundation for business success. We call this more rounded and honest understanding the *built-together reality* of individual and business success. In short, the built-together reality asserts that individual and business success is built through hard work but also taxpayer-supported schools, roads, and courts; the contributions of others; and chance factors like luck, historical timing, and various head starts in life.

In reclaiming the narrative of wealth creation, we could have filled the pages of this book with facts and figures drawn from the works of great economists, but facts alone stand little chance when pitted against a story that is so deeply embedded in our national character. From Horatio Alger to Ayn Rand, writers have told stories of individual and business success, complete with heroes and villains. In doing so they have sold a message to the broad public, a public that would likely never read the writings of conservative economists like Milton Friedman. Stories, unlike facts and data points, define our culture. They establish values and deeply held beliefs that facts alone cannot refute.

As a result, this book draws primarily from the first-person real-life stories of entrepreneurs, business leaders, and other high-wealth individuals, using their own words. Through their stories, and a few facts we included for good measure, we seek to establish a more balanced understanding of the true sources of individual wealth and business success. Their stories paint a much different picture than the self-made myth. In addition to the importance of hard work, creativity, and short-term sacrifice to their business success, they talk of the contributions of co-founders, colleagues, and employees; the role public investments play in wealth building; the role of government rules and regulations that provide a stable framework for business to operate and thrive; and additional factors such as inheritance, privilege, and luck. This is the essence of the built-together reality.

One of the entrepreneurs featured in this book is Jerry Fiddler, founder of the tech company Wind River Systems, which employed more than 1,600 workers when it was sold to Intel in 2009 for $884 million.[6] The company makes embedded software for an array of electronic devices, from car ignitions to digital cameras and even NASA's Mars Rover. Fiddler, who now serves as principal of Zygote Ventures, understands the role that public investments played both in his own success and in that of his business.

> Wind River wouldn't have existed without government-funded research that I did at Lawrence Berkeley Laboratories. I wouldn't have gotten that job at the lab if I hadn't had a master's degree. I wouldn't have had a master's or a bachelor's degree if there weren't a public university that provided me with financial aid. And if I hadn't gone to a good high school, also public, I probably wouldn't have gotten *into* the university.
>
> So, do I, as a successful business owner in the US, owe some of that back to society at some point? Absolutely, yes. . . .
>
> Like any successful business owner, I worked very hard, and I was also lucky. A lot of other people also worked hard and contributed sweat and ideas to build Wind River. And my employees and I benefited from a whole system of public and private benefits—laws and enforcement, financial incentives, education, research, infrastructure, national defense—the list goes on, and all of these things are supported by tax dollars.[7]

Jean Gordon, a small-business owner in Little Rock, Arkansas, tells a similar story. Her family business, Frostyaire of Arkansas, employs 45 people who freeze and store food, primarily chicken, for food processors and wholesale and retail food businesses, with cold storage food freezers in Batesville and Maumelle, Arkansas. She spoke at a press conference organized by United for a Fair Economy and Responsible Wealth in 2010, declaring, "My family members agree with me. . . . Frostyaire's success depends on government investments like good public schools that give us well-educated employees, and good highways so our customers can ship food."

Gordon goes on to talk not just about the public investments that have benefited her family business but also the role a strong middle class, supported through public policies, has played in keeping her business profitable. "At Frostyaire, our decisions about hiring employees, purchasing equipment, and expanding the business are not based on tax policy but on the number of customers and the amount of product they have to store with us. . . . The best way to help small businesses like ours is to put more money in the hands of the middle class who will spend the money as customers of our businesses . . ."[8]

Gordon's testimonial echoes the writings of economist and former Secretary of Labor Robert Reich. Reich argues that is it no accident that our nation's most vibrant period of economic growth took place when our middle class was strongest.[9] It is this middle class, and the public policies that support and strengthen it, that allows businesses like Gordon's to prosper and grow.

In story after story throughout this book, the entrepreneurs we have profiled point to factors beyond themselves that helped their businesses succeed. There is no doubt that an entrepreneurial spirit is important, but it is not enough by itself. The public structures that we as a society built together, through governmental action—including roads, courts, schools, parks, and more—are like the soil rich in nutrients in which the seeds of prosperity and entrepreneurship take root. If the soil is neglected and becomes rocky and barren, the seeds stand little chance of germinating or of reaching their full potential if they do survive. Warren Buffett, founder of Berkshire Hathaway, made this very point in a television interview: "I personally think that society is responsible for a very significant percentage of what I've earned. If you stick me down in the middle of Bangladesh or Peru or someplace, you'll find out how much this talent is going to produce in the wrong kind of soil. I will be struggling 30 years later. I work in a market system that happens to reward what I do very well—disproportionately well."[10]

We couldn't agree more. We applaud the leadership of Warren Buffett, and the many other business leaders profiled in this book, in helping us move toward a more honest assessment of individual wealth and success and, in doing so, providing greater clarity about the major policy choices facing us today.

Implications of the Built-Together Reality and the Public Investment Imperative It Supports

By acknowledging the various factors contributing to wealth creation, the built-together reality lays the foundation for a more honest debate about the issues of our time. The built-together reality acknowledges the way public investments in our shared prosperity lift us all, including entrepreneurs and business leaders. By this view government plays an important role in building a foundation upon which individual and business success is possible, by investing in schools, transportation, and more; by sowing the seeds of innovation; and by ensuring stable rules of the road. With the built-together reality and the public investment imperative that flows from it in clear view, our views on a host of issues and policy choices shift in dramatic ways.

If random luck, historical timing, inheritance, and race play a significant role in individual and business success, then the moral justification for extreme inequality evaporates. At the same time, if public investments in transportation infrastructure, schools and universities, research and innovation, as well as courts and a stable business environment are significant contributors to the success of those at the top, then progressive taxes are no longer about "punishing success" but rather about giving back to support the nation and the states that helped make their wealth possible.

If investments in the common good are an important part of the financial success of business leaders and entrepreneurs, then anti-government attempts to make government as small as possible are in fact shortsighted and damaging. Instead we would be well served to make needed investments in a wide array of public structures, from the next generation of transportation and energy systems to an education system that sows the seeds of prosperity for generations to come. Instead of cutting taxes on "job creators," the built-together reality suggests we should invest in America and revitalize Main Street, the underpinnings of any successful business.

If, as the built-together reality suggests, the success of those at the top is in part the result of others, including their employees, then organizing efforts to secure fair wages are morally justified. Similarly, if the misfortune of those struggling to make ends is the result not of laziness or sloth but of a plant's closing or health issues beyond their control (i.e., bad luck), then today's assault on the social safety nets is unnecessarily punitive. In fact, there is evidence that social safety nets actually *increase* people's ability to overcome systemic barriers and rise to success in business and in the community.

Digging Deeper

It is in this spirit of shifting the public debate in transformational ways that we open this book with an examination of the self-made myth, its roots and modern forms, and its implications. From there we seek to reclaim a more honest narrative of individual and business success—that of the built-together reality—and to shift the way we think about the big public policy questions of our day.

The Self-Made Myth

Origins of the Self-Made Myth

The myth of the self-made man lies deep in our country's collective psyche. As a new nation breaking free of its colonial ruler, America's identity was built in large part on the contrast of our frontier nation—with farmers carving a living out of the raw wilderness and merchants peddling their wares on our city streets— with that of Europe, whose economic pecking order was still largely defined by one's pedigree and aristocratic lineage. Though this contrast was at times exaggerated, it nonetheless helped shape our identity as a new nation.

Many of our nation's Founders viewed the concentrated and hereditary wealth of Europe's aristocracies as incompatible with the democracy they were trying to create in the United States. To ensure that our nation charted a different course, Thomas Jefferson and others championed the distribution of federally acquired land to small-scale yeoman farmers who would work the land themselves. This system of broadly distributed wealth was viewed as more consistent with the values of the emerging democracy.[1]

Others echoed this aversion to concentrated wealth. In 1765 John Adams said, "Property monopolized or in possession of a few is a curse to mankind." As one writer recently noted, "Adams knew that too much power in the hands of a wealthy powerful few would be detrimental to mankind, and in America today, the curse to mankind is the few monopolizing the resources of the majority."[2]

It was in this new, more equal nation that aristocratic lineage and pedigree were no longer the measure of one's worth. Instead a man's rise and fall was, in principle at least, due to his own merit, character, and hard work. With the trappings of bloodlines and aristocracy swept aside, the stage was set for the emergence of the "self-made" man in America.

During our nation's early history, a new type of self-help literature emerged, celebrating the personal qualities one must develop to better oneself and achieve prosperity. Benjamin Franklin's famous *Poor Richard's Almanac* was filled with such advice for poor Americans looking to get ahead.

By the nineteenth century, scores of writers, religious pulpits, schools, and penny presses built on Franklin's legacy, churning out the gospel of individual success. One of these "preachers" was Horatio Alger, the Harvard-educated novelist and former minister who churned out more than 100 such pieces, from short stories to novels such as *Ragged Dick*. His stories told a formulaic narrative of the poor boy who rose from rags to riches as a result of hard work and individual character. Young boys and men across the nation read these books, and those of others, for guidance and advice on how they too could become rich and successful.

In addition to the moralistic novels of Alger and others, there were real-life stories, told in news articles around the country, of millionaires who seized their piece of success through steady application to business. In some cases, though certainly not all, they rose up from working-class roots to do so. Together these various success stories worked to fuel the self-made myth.

There were skeptics, however, who questioned the self-made myth. The humorist Mark Twain reveled in turning the Alger story on its head[3] with "The Story of the Bad Little Boy Who Did Not Come to Grief" in 1865, "The Story of the Good Little Boy Who Did Not Prosper" in 1870, and "Poor Little Stephen Girard" in 1879, among others. In classic Twain fashion, these stories poked fun at the improbable rags-to-riches narrative and its moralizing of success. Despite following all the advice of Alger and his ilk, the "good boys" in Twain's stories were chased away by the business owner[4] or, worse, blown to smithereens.[5] The "bad boy" ended up wealthy and successful.[6]

Beyond the moralizing ridiculed by Twain, this individual success myth overlooked a number of key social and environmental factors. The emergence of a clear geography of opportunity showed that there was something about the place where one lived that contributed to one's success. No matter what personal qualities someone had, if you lived in Appalachia or the South, your chances of ascending the ladder to great wealth were slim. Those who achieved great wealth were almost invariably from the bustling industrial cities of the Northeast. By one estimate, three out of four millionaires in the nineteenth century were from New England, New York, or Pennsylvania.[7]

Another unique external factor was the opportunity that existed at that time, thanks to expanding frontiers and seemingly unlimited natural resources. The United States was conquering and expropriating land from native people and distributing it to railroads, White homesteaders, and land barons. Most of the major Gilded Age fortunes were tied to cornering a market and exploiting natural resources such as minerals, oil, and timber. Even P. T. Barnum, the celebrated purveyor of individual success aphorisms, had to admit in *Art of Money Getting* that "in the United States, where we have more land than people, it is not at all difficult for persons in good health to make money."[8]

He might have added that it also helped to be male, to be free rather than a slave, and to be White. While free Blacks had some rights in the North, they had little opportunity to achieve the rags-to-riches dream because of both informal and legal discrimination. Even after the Civil War, Blacks, Asians, and others were largely excluded from governmental programs like the Homestead Act that distributed an astounding 10 percent of all US lands—270 million acres—to 1.6 million primarily White homesteaders.[9]

Then there was the luck of timing. Those born in the first half of the nineteenth century who survived the Civil War caught the wave of resource exploitation and industrial expansion. This was the time of railroads and the dawn of Wall Street. Of the 75 richest people in all human history, 14 were Americans born between 1831 and 1840, including John D. Rockefeller, Jay Gould, J. P. Morgan, Frederick Weyerhaeuser, and Andrew Carnegie.[10] Historian Irvin Wyllie notes that from a statistical point of view, being born in 1835 was "the most propitious birth year for a poor boy who hoped to rise into the business elite."[11] Carnegie hit this lottery perfectly. He was born in 1835, held a desk job during the Civil War, and reached business maturity after the fighting ceased.

Finally, it's also clear that the majority of nineteenth-century millionaires were not in fact born poor but came from middle-class or wealthy households.[12] With so many reasons to doubt the validity of the self-made myth, it's no surprise that political scientist Francis Leiber declared in 1882, "Self made men, indeed! Why don't you tell me of the self-laid egg?"[13]

By the turn of the century, the rags-to-riches story began to lose its influence. "Soothsayers could not conceal the fact that the frontier had closed, that the nation's basic resources had long since been appropriated, and that small enterprisers had been put on the defensive by big business[;] . . . competition for top positions became more severe, [and] employers raised standards of qualifications by requiring degrees . . ."[14] Education, once regarded as optional and even detrimental to financial success, became a prerequisite for top positions in the newly organized, large-scale enterprises. Access to advanced education, however, often mirrored preexisting class differences and thus eroded the avenues for poor Americans to advance.

By the 1920s the post–World War I prosperity briefly reinvigorated the self-help credo. The modified formula for success now included professional training and an understanding of modern psychology in addition to character and hard work. But the

Depression put a dent in this success ideology. Wyllie writes, "As virtuous men took their places in the breadlines, silence fell over many of the sages who had vouched for the doctrine of wealth through virtue."[15]

By the middle of the twentieth century, scholars like C. Wright Mills were explaining the societal roots of success and poverty. This social science approach to understanding mobility, success, and opportunity found growing support. Nonetheless the myth of the self-made man has great potency to this day. In explaining wealth and success, the practice of elevating individual character while ignoring social and environmental factors is an enduring national tendency.

Modern Myth and the Titans of Industry

As industries have become organized on a larger scale, as technology has evolved and the world has become more interconnected, the role of the individual business leader has become increasingly intertwined with that of the larger society around us. Nonetheless the self-made myth persists and in some ways has even grown in influence, holding sway over our political and cultural debates.

With the tax debate intensifying in recent years, it has become infused at every turn with the self-made myth. Conservative talk-radio shows regularly use phrases like "punishing success" when referring to rolling back the Bush tax cuts for top income-earners. The assertion here is that it is *their* success and their success alone. Within the "punishing success" frame, there is no acknowledgment that others, whether co-workers, society, or taxpayers (who paid for the roads and the schools and the courts that businesses rely on), had anything to do with that success.

Similarly, the rhetoric of the self-made man is evident in the debates over the extravagant and sometimes controversial CEO pay. When the then-CEO of Scott Paper, "Chainsaw" Al Dunlap, who was later disgraced after he engineered a massive accounting

scandal at Sunbeam-Oster,[16] was asked on *PBS News Hour* to justify his $100 million pay package, he declared, "I created six and
a half billion [dollars] of value . . . I received less than 2 percent of
the value I created."[17]

Similarly, Dennis Kozlowski, the indicted former CEO of Tyco
International, was asked to justify his $170 million pay package
in 1999, which was second on the annual *Businessweek* executive
compensation list.[18] He responded, "I created about $37 billion in
shareholder value."[19] There was no mention of the share of wealth
created by the company's other 180,000 employees.

The operative word in each of these stories is *I*. Not one of these
modern-day CEO heroes mentioned the share of wealth created by
the thousands of employees at his company. To acknowledge the
other people and the complex factors contributing to the CEOs'
wealth might loosen their claim to bloated compensation packages.

To understand the ideological turn the self-made myth has
taken in recent decades, it's helpful to look at the recent popularity of the writings of novelist Ayn Rand among conservative
ideologues. While economists like Milton Friedman drove the
rightward shift on the academic side, Rand's novels, most notably
Atlas Shrugged, provided the narratives, complete with heroes and
villains, that are essential to cultural myth-making.

It's hard to overestimate the significance of Rand's writing in
guiding far-right thinking in the United States. Congressman Paul
Ryan stated in an ad, "Ayn Rand more than anyone else did a fantastic job of explaining the morality of capitalism, the morality of
individualism, and this to me is what matters most."[20]

Stephen Moore wrote in the *Wall Street Journal*, "Some years
ago when I worked at the libertarian Cato Institute, we used to
label any new hire who had not yet read *Atlas Shrugged* a 'virgin.'
Being conversant in Ayn Rand's classic novel about the economic
carnage caused by big government run amok was practically a
job requirement."[21]

In an on-air rant, Rush Limbaugh echoes Rand—whom he calls a "brilliant writer and novelist"[22]—arguing, "When you vote for politicians who take from your back pocket to give to others, you think it's compassionate, you think it's caring? It's not. It's depriving the recipient of his own quest for self-interest."[23] The quest to serve one's own self-interest above all else is a central tenet of Rand's philosophy.

The popularity of Rand has seeped into the Tea Party movement as well. The *Christian Science Monitor* writes, "At tea party meetings in September, Rand's name competed in popularity with Jefferson. Some demonstrations even started with a reading from *Atlas Shrugged,* which was coupled with the declaration that this book should be treated as 'America's Second Declaration of Independence.'"[24]

Like the propagandists of the nineteenth century, there are those who are doing all they can to spread the Rand worldview, including the banker John Allison, former chair of BB&T Company. According to a recent *Bloomberg* article, "Allison, working through the BB&T Charitable Foundation, gives schools grants of as much as $2 million if they agree to create a course on capitalism and make Rand's masterwork, *Atlas Shrugged,* required reading."[25] Despite the objections of professors and others who are concerned about the power of wealthy donors to dictate course curriculum, at least 60 schools, including several major universities, have accepted the grants and are now teaching Rand's work.[26]

The cumulative effect of this recent interest, along with Allison's bankrolling, can be seen in the sales figures for *Atlas Shrugged.* Though the book has sold 7 million copies since it was first published in 1957, an astounding 500,000 of those copies were sold in 2009 alone. That was twice the previous annual sales record set in 2008.[27]

So who is Ayn Rand, and what did she stand for? Whereas Horatio Alger embodied the self-made man myth of the nineteenth century, perhaps Ayn Rand best captures that myth taken to its extreme in the twentieth and twenty-first centuries. While both authors lifted up the accomplishments of the individual with a blind eye to the contributions of society, they differed in significant ways, most notably in their views of altruism and religion (Rand abhorred both).[28] Unlike Alger, Rand argues that any exertion of effort to serve others, whether God or the community at large, is a violation of the moral obligation to seek one's own self-interest above all else.[29]

Despite the controversial nature of Rand's writings on morality, her view of entrepreneurs and industrialists has grown in popularity and captures the self-made man story taken to its extreme. In *Atlas Shrugged* the industrialists and the business leaders, fed up with what they view as government intervention and meddling in their affairs, ironically go on "strike," retreating to a secret hideaway. In the subsequent years, the nation descends into chaos and riots as the economy, absent the leadership of these great men, grinds to a halt. Eventually, after the world has learned the folly of its ways, the industrialists return from their secret hideaway.

The essential message of *Atlas Shrugged* is that our nation owes a debt of gratitude to the heroic entrepreneurs, business leaders, and industrialists whose ingenuity, brilliance, leadership, risk-taking, and hard work are the wellsprings from which all prosperity flows. Without them our nation would fall apart. Government gets in the way or, worse, saps private-sector productivity through public policies to protect and benefit the undeserving.

Recent statements from the likes of House Republican Conference Chairman Jeb Hensarling (R-TX) echo Rand's worldview: "Americans know full well that you can't help the job seeker by punishing the job creator."[30] Embodied in that statement is the glorification of business leaders as "job creators" as well as the subservient relationship the rest of America has to them. It captures the essence of the world described by Rand, a world that consists of two basic groups: industrious job creators and everyone else.

While the nineteenth-century version of the self-made myth, popularized by Horatio Alger and others of his ilk, differs in notable ways from Ayn Rand's mythical titans of industry, they contain some key commonalities. Most notably, both variants pay little or no attention to external factors, especially the contributions of society, that may have contributed to the success of these so-called self-made men. In short, they assert that the success of entrepreneurs and business leaders is entirely their own doing.

Fueling an Anti-government Narrative

The self-made myth is evident in the political dialogues of the day. It has served as a political tool to fuel an anti-government narrative, eroding public support for that which we build together as a society.

Just days after Barack Obama's proposed $2 trillion deficit reduction plan was released in September 2011, House Speaker John Boehner issued a written statement, citing the "administration's insistence on raising taxes on job creators" as the reason he could not come to agreement with the president on a deficit reduction plan.[31] In Boehner's statement is the "job creators" frame again—that is, the heroic individuals at the top of our economy, who by themselves are responsible not only for their own success but for creating jobs and lifting up the national economy as a whole, like Rand's Atlas.

From there it's a short leap to the anti-government narrative. The title of one recent editorial, "How Big Gov't Strangles the Job Creators," says it all.[32] If all wealth (and jobs) derive entirely from the self-made titans of industry and finance, there is no room for government. In fact, government only gets in the way. That is the frame. That is the operating assumption for those who elevate the self-made myth and its companion, the anti-government narrative, as gospel. This anti-government narrative has been used to justify deregulation of financial markets, the stripping away of public safety standards, and the weakening of environmental protection enforcement. This anti-government narrative has also been used to justify deep cuts to education, financial aid, transportation, and a wide range of public supports essential to a functioning democracy and a healthy economy. It is the operating assumption behind the *cuts-only* solution to the budget crisis being advocated by some in Washington and in state houses across the nation.

Furthermore, if one accepts that the wealth of successful individuals is entirely their own doing, vast inequalities of wealth can be rationalized away as simply the result of their hard work and brilliance. Government should do nothing to intervene. Extravagant CEO pay can be justified because "they created" enormous shareholder value. Efforts of workers to organize for a fair wage may be viewed as extortion from the titans of industry who created the wealth. Under such a frame, taxes, and especially progressive taxes, are akin to governmental theft of the hard-earned profits of successful individuals. Conservative think tanks like the Cato Institute frequently use the phrase "punishing success" when they speak of progressive taxes,[33] a recurring frame in our public dialogues today.

The acceptance of the myth also works to exacerbate our perceptions of race and class in society. Harlon L. Dalton of Yale University argues that the Horatio Alger myth "suggests that success in life has nothing to do with pedigree, race, class background, gender, national origin, sexual orientation—in short, with anything beyond our individual control. Those variables may exist, but they play no appreciable role in how our actions are appraised."[34] If, in fact, anyone can achieve financial success through industry and sound character, it may be argued that those who have not succeeded are therefore lazy or dishonest. By denying the role of racism, sexism, and even classism (and this list could be expanded), one can marginalize whole groups of people based on their lack of progress in achieving financial success.

Though we don't deal with it in this book, it's worth mentioning briefly an additional impact that the self-made myth has on our public debates—that of people voting their aspirations. Because the rags-to-riches myth persists, many Americans hold on to the belief, however unlikely, that they too may one day become wealthy. This has at times led to people's voting their aspirations rather than their reality. As Michael Moore noted in 2003:

> After fleecing the American public and destroying the American Dream for most working people, how is it that, instead of being drawn and quartered and hung at dawn at the city gates, the rich got a big wet kiss from Congress in the form of a record tax break, and no one says a word? How can that be? I think it's because we're still addicted to the Horatio Alger fantasy drug. Despite all the damage and all the evidence to the contrary, the average American still wants to hang on to this belief that maybe, just maybe, he or she (mostly he) just might make it big after all.[35]

It is essential that we find a more honest and complete narrative of wealth creation. In chapter 2, we expose the fallacy of the self-made myth by examining the stories of individuals often lifted up as successes in our public dialogues. In examining their stories, we come to better understand that even their business success includes contributions from society, from government, from other individuals, and even luck.

CHAPTER 2

Busting the Myth

Making the Invisible Visible

Americans are largely unaware of the very government benefits they personally receive. This fact was highlighted in a 2008 study by Cornell University professor Suzanne Mettler. She began her study by asking respondents if they had "ever used a government social program or not," and then later asked about a specific list of 19 programs.

The results of her study are telling. About 60 percent of those who benefited from home mortgage interest deduction and lifetime learning tax credits said they had never used a government social program, while 53 percent of those who received student loans claimed to have never used a government social program. Even more surprising, between 40 and 44 percent of those who had received Social Security, Pell Grants, unemployment insurance, Veterans Benefits, the GI Bill, or Medicare claimed to have never used a government social program.[1]

This blindness to society's role in all our lives has profound impacts on our public debates. Sara Robinson, Senior Fellow with the Campaign for America's Future, asks rhetorically about the Mettler study and the self-made myth this blindness supports:

> Did Mr. Self-Made Man grow up in a VA or FHA-funded house? Attend a public school or college? Go to school on the GI Bill, Pell Grants, or student loans? Does he claim a mortgage interest

tax deduction every year? Does he support his retired parents out of pocket, or does Social Security do it for him? Does his employer get government contracts or subsidies that make his paycheck possible? Does his business depend on a sound currency, enforceable contracts, or reliable transportation systems? . . .

Forget gratitude; these social contract deniers insist loudly that none of that ever happened. At all. They pay taxes; but they've never seen a cent returned to them for anything. And they write their "self-made" myths accordingly.[2]

This blindness to the governmental structures and programs that support us in our day-to-day lives is a broad, societal problem. It undercuts support for the very programs and policies that are essential to building a strong middle class.

When this blindness is extended to those at the very top of the economic ladder, however, it has an even more insidious and damaging effect on our public discourse and the policies that flow from it. Extravagant CEO salaries and vast inequalities of income and wealth, when viewed through this self-made lens, are simply the result of the hard work and the exceptional intelligence of those at the top. Similarly, progressive tax policies, for those who believe that wealth is entirely self-made, become akin to "punishing success."

There are successful individuals who have forgotten the societal roots of their success or vigorously deny the role of social forces in their good fortune. They use inherited privilege or societal investment to get ahead yet work to eliminate opportunities for others.

There are people in America who won't admit how much wealth and advantage they've had; they've been dealt a royal flush. These are the people who reap the most from government subsidies, yet when it comes time to spend money to give equal opportunity to the rest of society, they pull up the ladder. They lecture others about hard work, individual virtue, and meritocracy while personally harvesting the benefits of private inheritances and public subsidies.

Gwendolyn Parker is the author of *Trespassing*, a memoir about her own journey as an African-American woman in the halls of corporate privilege. She was troubled by George W. Bush's self-characterization on the campaign trail that he was a successful businessman:

> How can George W. Bush, born into a family whose wealth and power and privilege far outstrip my own, not similarly see the truth about his own life? I wouldn't think less of Governor Bush if he just admitted that he'd been lucky, certainly very lucky, and left it at that. Few of us have led luckless lives, and there is neither merit nor shame in the truth.
>
> But I worry about a presidential candidate who feels compelled to re-form luck and privilege into primarily the sweat of his own brow. I worry particularly about how many American lives he'll need to misinterpret so that he can continue to tell the story he likes to tell about himself.[3]

If we are to have an honest debate about the important public policies of our day, we must clear away this self-made myth and view the world through a new frame. As Robinson argues, any real reform "must begin with explicitly making the invisible visible to the eyes of the public. . . . Nobody in America ever did it alone, for themselves. For the past 220 years, we've done it together, for each other. Bringing that interdependence back out into the light and putting it at the center of our politics shifts the entire dialogue."[4]

Only when people see the societal contributions to individual success—contributions made possible through governmental action—as well as the role of privilege and luck can we have an honest and productive debate about the public policies of the day.

In this chapter we examine the stories of high-wealth individuals and business leaders who are generally viewed by themselves or by society as self-made. In doing so we bust the self-made myth and make the invisible visible.

Donald Trump: FHA Housing, Imminent Domain, and Bank Bailouts

Donald Trump is the president of The Trump Organization, a business magnate, and a reality-television personality on The Apprentice.

Donald Trump is viewed by some as one of the shrewdest American business tycoons of his generation. In March 2011 *Forbes* estimated his net worth to be $2.7 billion, with a $60 million salary.[5] Many praise and analyze his "success" as if it were self-made, and they fail to attribute the proper credit to others in society where it is deserved. Despite what Trump may espouse, his success would have been in no way possible without his father, the general public, and the US government. Unfortunately, Trump decided to forget or selectively ignore these truths while forming his political philosophy, a sentiment made particularly clear during his brief bid for the 2012 Republican presidential nomination.

Trump was born in New York City in 1946, the son of real estate tycoon Fred Trump. Fred Trump's business success not only provided Donald Trump with a posh youth of private schools and economic security but eventually blessed him with an inheritance worth an estimated $40 million to $200 million.[6] It is critical to note, however, that his father's success, which granted Donald Trump such a great advantage, was enabled and buffered by governmental financing programs. In 1934, while struggling during the Great Depression, financing from the Federal Housing Administration (FHA) allowed Fred Trump to revive his business and begin building a multitude of homes in Brooklyn, selling at $6,000 apiece. Furthermore, throughout World War II, Fred

Trump constructed FHA-backed housing for US naval personnel near major shipyards along the East Coast.[7]

In 1974 Donald Trump became president of his father's organization. During the 15 years following his ascension, he expanded and innovated the corporation, buying and branding buildings, golf courses, hotels, casinos, and other recreational facilities. In 1980 he established The Trump Organization to oversee all of his real estate operations.[8]

Trump eventually found himself in serious financial trouble. In 1990, due to excessive leveraging, The Trump Organization revealed that it was $5 billion in debt ($8.8 billion by some estimates), with $1 billion personally guaranteed by Trump himself. The survival of the company was made possible only by a bailout pact agreed upon in August of that same year by some 70 banks, allowing Trump to defer on nearly $1 billion in debt, as well as to take out second and third mortgages on almost all of his properties.[9] If it were not for the collective effort of all banks and parties involved in that 1990 deal, Trump's business would have gone bankrupt and failed.

In 1995 Trump took Trump Hotels & Casino Resorts Inc. public and received a substantial financial boost from society and the Securities and Exchange Commission (SEC) regulations that enable the market to function. He initially sold 10 million shares at $14 per share and then in 1996 sold 13.25 million shares at $32.50 a share.[10] This initial public offering granted Trump's company a stability and legitimacy that would have been impossible without millions of people around the world trusting his organization and investing with the hope of shared success.

Despite the clear societal and governmental assistance described above, Trump continues to be outspoken in his criticism of government. In his book *The America We Deserve,* Trump explains that "the greatest threat to the American Dream is the idea that dreamers need close government scrutiny and control.

Job one for us is to make sure the public sector does a limited job, and no more."[11] This quote proves to be particularly ironic when considering Trump's feelings about eminent domain laws. He was quoted as saying, "I happen to agree with it 100 percent" when speaking of the 2005 Supreme Court decision on *Kolo v. New London,* which affirmed the government's ability to transfer land from one private owner to another for the purpose of economic development in the area.[12] In fact, Trump attempted to take advantage of eminent domain laws on multiple occasions, once even demanding that an elderly widow give up her home so that he could build a limousine parking lot.[13]

Perhaps more disturbing than his hypocritical condemnation of the government is his failure to acknowledge anyone's contributions, save his own, in the creation of his success. At the 2011 Conservative Political Action Conference, Trump made clear his feelings on the creation of his wealth: "Over the years I've participated in many battles and have really almost come out very, very victorious every single time. I've beaten many people and companies, and I've won many wars. I have fairly but intelligently earned many billions of dollars, which in a sense was both a scorecard and acknowledgment of my abilities."[14] Furthermore, Trump apparently sees no benefit in supporting taxes to maintain institutions such as the Securities and Exchange Commission to regulate the stock market, in which he publicly trades his company, or the court system, which actively protects his property rights: "We are the highest taxed nation—I would tax foreign countries that are ripping off the US and lower taxes for Americans."[15]

From the moment of his birth, Trump was set up for success. The large inheritance left to him by his father, coupled with the contributions and the protections of society and the US government made his ascension to the Forbes 400 list almost inevitable. Nevertheless, Trump fails to recognize this phenomenon and continues to express his belief that he did it alone.

H. Ross Perot Sr.: Medicare, Medicaid, and the Right Connections

H. Ross Perot Sr. founded Electronic Data Systems, was twice a presidential candidate, and as of 2011 was among the 100 wealthiest people in the United States.

H. Ross Perot Sr. is best known as a candidate for president. In his 1992 campaign, he ran as an independent, using $65.4 million of his own money, and won 19 percent of the vote.[16] He then started the Reform Party, under whose banner he ran again for president in 1996.[17] Though his political moment may have passed, he remains an economic powerhouse in America to this day. As of this writing, the 81-year-old Perot is one of the 100 richest individuals in the United States, with an estimated net worth of $3.4 billion.[18]

Perot was born in Texarkana, Texas, in June 1930. He attended public and private schools and Texarkana Junior College. Perot is largely regarded as a self-made billionaire. Even the profile on Forbes.com lists the source of his wealth as "computer services, real estate, *self-made* [emphasis added]."[19] His father, Gabriel Elias Perot, however, was a successful cotton broker in an area where cotton was king. Perot credited his father with giving him exposure to business. Although the Perots struggled during the Great Depression, the family owned a spacious home, attended a private country club, and sent Ross Perot and his sister to a private Christian grammar school.[20]

It was already clear at a young age that Ross Perot was highly disciplined, competitive, and hardworking. As a teenager he embarked on a number of jobs and entrepreneurial ventures. He entered the US Naval Academy in 1949 and was considered a natural leader among his peers.[21]

Perot left the US Navy and moved to Dallas, Texas, where he took a sales job at International Business Machines (IBM). By all accounts Perot was a quick learner and showed a great deal of initiative and innovation. While he was working with one IBM client, Texas Blue Cross, Perot identified a niche for a future business. He thought that IBM put too much focus on selling computers and not enough effort into helping clients use the machinery. "I realized that people did not want computers, they wanted the results that came from computers."[22]

In 1962 Perot founded Electronic Data Systems (EDS), a one-man data-processing company that went on to employ more than 70,000 people. But in its early days, EDS owned no computers and rented office space from Texas Blue Cross. The company struggled to make a profit in its early years. In 1964 it had earnings of $400,000 but made only $4,100 in profit.[23] But EDS was a company that was in the right place at the right time.

In July 1965 the US Congress passed legislation establishing the Medicare and Medicaid programs. A cornerstone of Lyndon Johnson's Great Society initiative, these insurance programs would entitle 30 million US citizens to health benefits.[24] This would in turn create an enormous volume of paperwork and an acute need for data-processing systems.

EDS moved into this enormous market, using its inside connection with Texas Blue Cross, the agency that would administer the federal program in Texas. Texas Blue Cross gave EDS its computer data business without any competitive bid. In its 1968 contract with Texas Blue Cross, EDS was paid $250,000 to develop a computer program to process Medicare claims. While government funds paid for research and development (R&D) of the system, EDS retained ownership of the program. Essentially, the R&D costs for EDS's main product were paid for with tax dollars.[25]

Gerald Posner, in his biography of Perot, called him the "Welfare Billionaire":[26] "The EDS program, developed with the help of Texas Blue Cross and paid for by federal funds, was the same one that Perot kept reselling at a significant profit to other states. . . . The issue was of no small consequence, because between 1966 and

1971 . . . the federal government paid EDS $36 million (the company had only $400,000 in revenues in 1964). Its closest competitor during the same time, Applied Systems Development Corporation, received just $275,000."[27]

The EDS Medicare contract was a windfall. There is no question that the early relationship with Texas Blue Cross helped build the company and enabled it to catch a veritable wave of opportunities.

In 1965, the first year of EDS's government contracts, revenues were $865,000 and profits were $26,487. By 1968 EDS had revenues of $7.5 million, with profits of $2.4 million.[28] While EDS's pretax profits were only 1 percent in 1964, they grew to 40 percent between 1966 and 1971. Government analysts estimated that in its Texas Medicare work, profit margins were more than 100 percent.[29] By 1971 EDS received $20.7 million of the $23.2 million paid to all Medicare subcontractors, or 90 percent of the market share.[30]

On September 12, 1968, the company went public. While the overwhelming majority of the company's business was tied to the Medicare program, the initial public-offering (IPO) prospectus represented the company as a diversified and well-rounded business. In the ensuing IPO buying frenzy, Perot's personal 10 million shares became worth $230 million overnight. At their peak in 1970, EDS shares traded at $162.50, putting Perot's personal net worth at more than $1.5 billion.[31] In 1984 Perot sold EDS to General Motors for $2.55 billion. Initially, Perot retained a large ownership interest in the company and a board seat at General Motors, but in 1986 GM bought out Perot's remaining stock for $700 million.[32]

Once established as one of the wealthiest men in the United States, Perot was easily able to stay on top. In 1988 he founded another information technology company, Perot Systems,[33] which he later sold to Dell for $3.9 billion in 2009, pocketing approximately $380 million for himself.[34]

The rise of Perot can no doubt be attributed in part to his many strong personal qualities. But looking at this simple biography, it is hard not to also see the contribution of other forces. These included fortunate timing, a virtual monopoly on a growing sector of government subcontracting, and public tax dollars subsidizing private research and development.

R E A L I T Y   C H E C K

Social Mobility and the Rags-to-Riches Story

Through most of our nation's history, writers telling the rags-to-riches story of so-called self-made men relied on anecdotal evidence or outright fiction. In recent decades social scientists have developed an array of tools, including "longitudinal data"—surveys that track the same families over multiple generations—to measure the veracity of the rags-to-riches story.

Social mobility describes the upward and downward mobility of individuals across generations, usually based on income, wealth, or occupational prestige. Income mobility, for example, is the likelihood of a person born to a family in the bottom of the income scale to move upward during his or her lifetime and someone born to a family at the top to move down the scale. Though the field is fairly new, and the data collection takes generations, some notable trends are emerging.

The first trend is that income mobility appears to be decreasing in the United States. That is, a person born to a low-income family today is more likely to stay low-income throughout life than 30 or 40 years ago when mobility was greater. This is especially pronounced in the past two decades.[35]

A second notable fact revealed in the social mobility data is that social mobility in many European nations is far higher than in the United States. In comparing the United States, Canada, and seven European nations, the United States and the United Kingdom have the lowest levels of social mobility. The highest levels of social mobility were in Denmark, Norway, Finland, and Canada. Sweden, Germany, and France fell in the middle.[36]

So why such a difference over time and among nations? Two factors are often cited in the literature. The first is an apparent link to inequality. In *The Spirit Level,* Richard Wilkinson and Kate Pickett write, "The relationship between intergenerational social mobility and income inequality is very strong . . . Countries with bigger income differences [like the United States and the United Kingdom] tend to have much lower social mobility."[37]

Jared Bernstein, Senior Fellow with the Center on Budget and Policy Priorities, pointing to the declining mobility in the United States, makes a similar assessment: "I predict that future research will find this slowdown [in mobility], and I strongly suspect there's a linkage between slower mobility and higher inequality."[38]

The second factor appears to be in the realm of social safety nets and investments in the common good. Evidence indicates that part of the international differences is attributable to the availability of higher education to those at all income levels. In their 2006 paper, Emily Beller and Michael Hout state, "Opportunity is much greater among college-educated adults of different class backgrounds than it is among adults with less education. The United States has one of the highest levels of college attendance, but also a relatively low level of equality in overall educational opportunity."[39]

In a similar vein, Bernstein writes about investments in public education, libraries, health care, and food/nutrition, including Head Start and the Special Supplemental Nutrition Program for Women, Infants, and Children (WIC): "These programs have been shown, in pretty extensive and consistent research, to be associated with lifelong advantages. . . . It shouldn't surprise us that greater social protections are associated with greater economic mobility. . . . They reduce increasingly entrenched societal barriers and thus enable people to better realize their intellectual and economic potential."[40]

After three decades of rising inequality, the United States now has the highest levels of income inequality the nation has seen since 1928, just before the Great Depression.[41] This rising inequality, coupled with the loss of public funding for education and investments in the common good, will only serve to further erode social mobility in the country, putting the rags-to-riches dream even further out of reach.

Koch Brothers: Money, Power, and Public Subsidies

David and Charles Koch are co-owners of Koch Industries, the second-largest privately held company in the United States, and major bankrollers of the Tea Party movement.

Money begets money, power accumulates, and the two elements tend to reinforce each other. The billionaire Koch brothers, who are behind much of the conservative intellectual and political ascendancy of the past 30 years, are among those lucky Americans who have enjoyed this self-perpetuating accumulation of influence. Like many of the super-wealthy, they preach a model of self-help in sharp variance with their own experience. But what makes them different from most of their hyper-affluent contemporaries is the aggressive way they've used their money and power to shape public policies that fit their self-serving ideology.

As with most family fortunes, the Koch brothers' money can be ascribed to many sources beyond their talents and hard work. Start with $300 million—as Charles and David Koch did when their father, the founder of what would become Koch Industries, died in 1967.[42] Before that, of course, the sons benefited from an upbringing that featured large homes, overseas travel, and the finest education at private schools, including the Massachusetts Institute of Technology, their father's alma mater.[43]

Despite spending hundreds of millions of dollars over the years demonizing government and promoting pure free-market capitalism, the Koch brothers have been unashamed recipients of corporate welfare. They graze cattle and harvest timber on public lands, reaping the profits while paying minuscule fees.[44] They use the government's power of eminent domain to obtain routes for their thousands of miles of gas and oil pipelines.[45] They even take advantage of direct government subsidies to produce ethanol.[46]

This last bit of public largesse is especially ironic, since ethanol subsidies are the kind of government spending that is a perennial target of the Cato Institute, a libertarian think tank backed by Charles Koch since its founding in 1977. Cato was the first of scores of such conservative institutes, advocacy groups, and campaigns the Koch brothers would bankroll over the years: well-known political actors like the Heritage Foundation and the Tea Party and lesser-known academic departments that quietly turn out conservative scholarship and conservative graduates year after year.[47]

In addition to bankrolling the intellectual underpinnings of conservatism, the Koch brothers also attempt to change public policy more directly by contributing millions of dollars to political candidates and committees. The vast majority goes to the GOP, including a number of successful state-level Republican candidates in 2010 who, once in office, set about cutting corporate taxes, weakening public services, and reducing the rights of public employees.[48]

Koch-funded critics of the Obama administration often denounce its policies as "socialist"; David Koch himself has described President Obama as a "hardcore socialist."[49] But the Koch brothers have no problem doing business with a *real* socialist when there is profit to be made: since 1998 they have been partners in a fertilizer factory with a state-run firm in Hugo Chavez's Venezuela, enjoying millions of dollars in socialist government subsidies every year.[50]

The Koch brothers' partnership with Chavez is really not surprising, given that their father's empire got its start in partnership with the world's most infamous communist, Joseph Stalin. Fred Koch—inventor of an improved method of deriving gasoline from oil—spent the 1930s growing rich in the Soviet Union while helping launch the Russian petroleum industry and fulfill Stalin's first Five-Year Plan.[51]

In 1991 David Koch was the only first-class passenger to survive a plane crash; during recovery he was diagnosed with prostate cancer.[52] He undoubtedly used his resources to ensure the best care and recovery possible from both misfortunes, as anyone would. But his experience was likely very different from that of someone who was dependent on the private health insurance industry to pay for medical treatment, or who was uninsured (President Obama recalls visiting his mother in the hospital during her final days fighting cancer and finding her on the phone arguing with her insurance company). And yet David Koch and his brother Charles financed, through their various front groups, an intense opposition to federal health-care reform that will enable millions of the uninsured to obtain coverage and curb the worst abuses of the health insurance industry. In other words, they fought reform that will, in essence, bring the health-care experiences of average Americans closer to what the Koch brothers are able to buy.

David Koch also sat on a government cancer advisory council even as the private advocacy groups he and his brother support lobbied against having formaldehyde—a profitable Koch Industries product—declared a carcinogen.[53]

In 2008 the two brothers were each individually included on a "Top 50" American charitable givers list compiled by *Businessweek*. The magazine described elder brother Charles's $246 million in philanthropy that year as targeting "libertarian causes, giving money for academic and public policy research and social welfare around strict conservative ideals."[54]

Younger brother David spreads his munificence with fewer obvious political aims, including among the beneficiaries educational and medical research (especially on prostate cancer). The Manhattan resident has also become a patron of the arts, serving on the board of the Metropolitan Museum of Art and paying to build the theater at Lincoln Center in which both the New York City Ballet and the Metropolitan Opera perform.[55]

Like many upper-income people, the Koch brothers disregard many sources of their great fortune—not only inherited wealth and direct public subsidies but the shared blessings of civilization, from public roads and public research to police and patents. The Kochs go further, though, in also disregarding the moderation called for in wielding the influence that flows from great personal wealth. They benefit from government generosity, both in the United States and abroad, then spend a portion of that money advocating for the elimination of public programs on which the working poor and the middle class depend. They oppose all campaign spending limits, allowing their huge expenditures to drown out the voices of ordinary Americans. They are perhaps a cautionary tale of how the intertwining vines of money and power, left unchecked, can threaten the very society from which they grow.

Summary: Cleaning the Slate

As we can see in these few examples, even some of the staunchest advocates of the self-made myth and the anti-government narrative it supports are themselves the beneficiaries of taxpayer-supported public investments, courts, and the legal framework made possible through governmental action. In many cases they are also the recipients of vast inheritances as well.

It's clear that these individuals cannot claim to have done it on their own. And there is no evidence that they rejected governmental support when it benefited them. Even Ayn Rand herself, despite a lifetime of railing against government, took Social Security payments and Medicare benefits under the name Ann O'Connor (her husband was Frank O'Connor).[56]

In making the invisible visible, these stories help shatter the self-made myth and the anti-government narrative it supports. With the myths and the hypocrisy brushed aside, recognized for what they are, we can now begin to build a new framework of individual and business success: the built-together reality.

CHAPTER 3

The Built-Together Reality of Individual Success

Roots of the Built-Together Reality

Is there an alternative to the self-made myth? Is there a more balanced narrative that honors the role of the individual while revealing a more accurate picture of the other factors of individual success? Yes. In our interviews and conversations with business leaders, entrepreneurs, and other high-wealth individuals, a more complex and honest story takes shape, what we call the built-together reality.

The understanding of our interconnectedness is deeply rooted in our society. Early in human history, people began to organize communities for mutual protection and shared well-being. From early Colonial pacts to the US Constitution, Americans have similarly recognized that we are all in this together, that no man is an island, and that our mutual prosperity is deeply intertwined. It is this deep and rich heritage that we draw upon when we lay out the framework of the built-together reality.

In articulating the built-together reality, we seek to find a balance that acknowledges both the contributions of the individual and the contributions of society, including those made possible through governmental action.

Role of Individual Effort and Leadership

There is no question that individual initiative, risk-taking, and creativity matter. Some people accumulate great wealth because of their extra effort and sacrifice. They have worked and saved while others have played and consumed. And they have taken real risks, betting the farm or home on a dream. Others succeed through effective leadership, which can infuse an organization with higher morale and productivity. Such leadership is often thankless and lonely, and the stress involved must seem, on many days, more trouble than it is worth.

Individual imagination and intelligence can transform an organization or an entire society. An innovative new idea to fill some unmet need can be a blessing for the community as a whole. The cotton gin, the assembly line, and the computer chip were technological advances with broad economic and social impacts in which individual inventors played a decisive role. Or consider how a piece of art, a song, or an evocative performance can move our hearts. We would be impoverished without these gifts to the world. Individuals should be rewarded for their contributions with social recognition and material benefit.

But how do we untangle the various threads of individual temperament, social privilege, and luck in any of our lives? We know that there are some individuals who seem to stand out because of their energy, creativity, or spark. But what about the role of the economic environment, historical timing, and public investments?

Biographies and the literature of success focus on the individual skills and qualities of business leaders and wealthy people. These qualities include maturity, a passionate drive for excellence, interpersonal and organizational skills, the ability to take initiative, and a willingness to delay personal gratification.

When asked about the forces that have shaped their success, many individuals point to personal factors in their own social upbringing and environment that made a difference. These include parental values; a supportive family and spouse; skilled and able co-workers; key mentors, teachers, and coaches; and perhaps a particular educational institution. Seldom will people go beyond personal factors and qualities to include broader contributors such as luck, timing, privileged upbringing, or the public resources on which their success is hinged. It is this latter set of factors that we now examine in more detail.

Unequal Opportunities and Historical Timing

While there is no doubt that starting a business in the United States gives one significant advantages, opportunity is not the same for all regardless of how hard they work or how diligently they apply the lessons of the purveyors of America's rags-to-riches narrative. If opportunity varies so dramatically, what does it mean for the self-made myth?

Historical Timing

We noted earlier the tremendous wave of opportunity that presented itself to those who were born in the 1830s and survived the Civil War. Andrew Carnegie, John D. Rockefeller, and many other nineteenth-century millionaires built their empires on the historic economic and industrial expansion of the time. Opportunity has continued to flow and ebb throughout our nation's history. The cause of that ebb and flow is rarely random, however, and frequently is the result of public policy choices of that time in history.

In 1921 Lewis Terman of Stanford University began what Malcolm Gladwell calls "one of the most famous psychological studies in history."[1] Using IQ tests, he sorted through 250,000 elementary and high school students to identify the top 1,470 "geniuses" with IQs of 140 and over. Then he began the lifelong task of tracking these geniuses over the course of their lives.[2] Though they all had comparable levels of "innate ability," they faced very different prospects in life for a variety of reasons. On timing, the "failures" in Terman's study were far more likely to be among those born between 1903 and 1911. It was they who had the unfortunate timing of entering the workforce during the worst of the Great Depression. What careers they did build were interrupted by the draft of World War II. The group born between 1912 and 1917, on the other hand, came of age after the worst of the Depression was over and entered World War II at a young enough age that the draft presented an opportunity more than a career interruption.[3]

Similarly, as the personal computer revolution took off in 1975, Bill Gates (b. 1955), Paul Allen (b. 1953), Steve Jobs (b. 1955), Bill Joy (b. 1954), Eric Schmidt (b. 1955), and other software giants were just coming of age, poised to build their computer empires. Had they been born a few years before, they would likely have ended up in the soon-to-be-outdated world of mainframes. If they had been born later, the historic window of opportunity would have already closed.[4] They were born at just the right time.

The fact is, when you were born matters a lot more than many would like to admit. Jim Sherblom, former chief financial officer (CFO) of Genzyme, notes how different his life prospects were from those of young Americans just entering the workforce today: "This Great Recession of 2008 is different than any other financial catastrophe that happened during my working career. We are going to be a very different society with very different expectations about what is possible for a young ambitious person who wants to do well in their life." Timing matters.

Random Luck

Billionaire oilman John Paul Getty once famously stated that his secret to success was to "Rise early, work hard, strike oil."[5] For those seeking to follow his advice, rising early and working hard are completely within their control. The good fortune of striking oil, though, points to the importance of luck in whether one person succeeds and another does not.

If luck is in fact a major factor in determining who is wealthy and who is not, then it casts into doubt the moral justification of the vast inequalities of income and wealth in our society. When the founder of Sears and Roebuck, Julius Rosenwald, attributed his success primarily to luck, he heard audible complaints. A trade journalist retorted, "If financial success was chiefly a matter of luck, there would be strong grounds for the surtaxes that governments so savagely levy on large incomes, for the voraciousness of unionized labor, and for the leveling process of Socialistic doctrine."[6] In other words, keep telling them it's your character. If they think it's luck, there may be social claims on your money. Of course, Getty also had the benefit of being White and male and of living in a nation that protects property rights. He was also born to a family in the petroleum business,[7] giving him a substantial head start on his career.

Class and Cultural Capital

Turning to the Terman geniuses again, we see the importance of class in shaping one's prospects in life. Terman divided 730 of the men, now adults, into three groups from the most successful to the least successful (top 20 percent, middle 60 percent, and bottom 20 percent). It became apparent that the family's background, that is, class, was the most important factor in determining a man's success. The top group overwhelmingly came from middle- and upper-class households where they had books, parents with college degrees, and ample resources to pursue their goals. The bottom group came from the other side of the tracks, lacking high-quality education, financial wherewithal, contacts, and role models. Again, these were all geniuses with the same "innate ability," but their life paths were very different because of the economic class into which they were born.[8]

In addition to the cultural capital that comes with class are the financial boosts one gets from one's parents. Gifts from parents to pay for higher education or a down payment on a home or to help start a business can transform a person's options and change a life trajectory. According to New York University sociologist Dalton Conley, the single most important factor in determining a young adult's net worth is the net worth of his or her parents.[9]

Among the very wealthy, inherited privilege is often a guaranteed catapult to continued wealth. Over one-third of the Forbes 400 in 1997, for instance, were born onto the list. Using baseball imagery, they essentially were born rounding third base and heading for home. And at least another quarter were born standing on the base path, meaning they were fortunate enough to inherit a small business, a piece of land with oil under it, or an investment of "parental equity" on flexible terms.[10] Each of these individuals contributed something unique, but they had a significant boost that someone born in the batter's box doesn't have. In the words of Seagrams billionaire Edgar Bronfman, "To turn $100 into $110 is work. To turn $100 million into $110 million is inevitable."[11]

Societal Barriers of Race and Gender

It is hard to discuss race in America without discussing economic class. While there have been great strides in achieving legal rights for Blacks and other communities of color, little has changed in the economic order. Many decades after the great Civil Rights victories were achieved, Blacks still hold only 10 cents of net wealth to every dollar of White median family net wealth. Latinos do not fare much better at 12 cents to every White dollar of net wealth.[12] Unlike income, wealth is readily transferred from one generation to the next through inheritance and other intergenerational transfers, ensuring that the inequalities of yesterday are carried forward to each successive generation despite progress made on other fronts.

This lack of net wealth has been a significant barrier to the emergence of Black-owned businesses. Robert Fairlie of the

University of California, Santa Cruz, documents the trend. "Blacks have made fair gains in the labor market, education, politics, and legal issues, but it seems to me like business ownership and performance are areas that have not seen the kind of progress that we've seen elsewhere."[13] Fairlie places the blame on the low level of personal wealth, which means limited access to startup capital for a new business. While Thomas Boston of the Georgia Institute of Technology takes a more optimistic view on the progress, he too acknowledges that lack of wealth is one of the main barriers to Black entrepreneurship.[14]

However you look at it, without wealth it is very difficult for anyone to break into the business world. This applies not just to Black would-be entrepreneurs but to Latinos, women, and others as well. So what does this mean for the rags-to-riches myth if it takes significant wealth to start a new business? What does it mean for the self-made myth if people of color, who don't have the same wealth at the starting line as Whites do, are less able to turn their entrepreneurial visions into reality?

Beyond the question of business ownership, race and gender discrimination are still pervasive problems in our society. Even in the regular workforce, there are still well-documented gaps in pay and professional advancement.[15] Our society goes even further by rewarding those whom it deems physically attractive or fitting the right image of success. A 2003 study concluded that tall people on average earn more money than short people, with each inch of height being equivalent to $789 a year in extra pay.[16]

Society's Contributions to Individual Success

In thinking about the interplay of the individual and society in building a successful business, it's helpful to think of a musician performing in a large arena. What we build together through generations of public investments in the common good—roads, education system, courts, a stable economic framework, publicly funded research, and much more—are like the stage, arena, and, most importantly, the PA system that amplifies the entrepreneur's creation. Without that infrastructure the musician, no matter how creative and talented, would have only limited reach.

The truth is that we have a robust economy precisely because we have an infrastructure that supports it. We have order and stability, a predictable system of rules for ownership and investing, and mechanisms to resolve disputes. Investors and entrepreneurs have confidence that the rules today will be the same next year and the year after. And we have a skilled workforce thanks to our nation's substantial investment in public education. That is the essence of the built-together reality.

Public Infrastructure

Entrepreneurs and business leaders in America rely on a wealth of public infrastructure—including roads, schools, parks, and more—paid for through our tax system. What's more, these commonly held assets accumulate over time thanks to generations of such public investments. It is upon these commonly held assets that entrepreneurs are able to build their business enterprises.

The individuals featured in this book, and many others whom we have interviewed, speak to the role that our nation's transportation infrastructure—including highways, airports, railroads, and seaports—plays in making their businesses possible (see "Reality Check: Highways and Transportation" in chapter 4). Most also speak to the importance of our public education system, which in many cases benefited them personally but which also provides their businesses with an educated workforce. This public infrastructure also extends to our communications networks, the Internet, and more.

In a 2004 report titled *Rethinking Growth Strategies,* economist Robert G. Lynch looked at a host of data and surveys on factors that drive economic growth and business location choices among states. He found that education of the local workforce and the transportation infrastructure, for example, were far more important than low taxes in determining business location. Lynch summarizes his findings: "There is evidence . . . that increases in taxes, when used to expand the quantity and quality of public services, can promote economic development and employment growth."[17] This finding is clearly reflected in the interviews we conducted with business leaders for this book.

Public Investment in Research and Innovation

As taxpayers we should be proud that the US government is the biggest venture capitalist in the world. The federal government spends more than a hundred billion dollars per year on research, mostly in grants to universities.[18] And public support doesn't stop once the technology has been developed. The US government also offers tax breaks to companies that invest in using technology. We should not underestimate the role of this research in creating the bedrock for wealth creation and the quality of life we enjoy.

Earlier in our nation's history, our government invested in the creation of agricultural extension agencies to spread new technologies and increase production of America's farmlands. In 1919, driven by national security concerns that Britain and Germany would dominate international radio, the Woodrow Wilson administration created the Radio Corporation of America (RCA) as a consortium to retain and develop crucial radio technology. "The firm that soon became America's leading consumer-electronics company was launched by government, and with an injection of public capital."[19] In 1915 Congress created the Advisory Committee for Aeronautics to jump-start America's aviation industry after it was clear that the United States was falling behind. One of its first projects was the creation of a giant wind tunnel to test different wing designs.[20]

Beginning in the mid-1960s, publicly funded R&D under the Defense Advanced Research Projects Agency began the process of creating what we all know today as the Internet (see "Reality Check: Building the Internet" in chapter 4). At the same time, government's tremendous buying power helped drive down the cost of microchips, making them affordable for consumers. The Breakthrough Institute writes, "Government procurement drove the price of microchips down by a factor of 50 in just a matter of years. Consider this: without these public investments in the semiconductor revolution, your iPod would cost $10,000 and be the size of a room!"[21] More recently, after extensive federal dollars and research grants, scientists successfully mapped the human genome, making possible a whole new wave of medical breakthroughs.[22]

All of these represent public actions that helped fuel innovation and our broader prosperity. Government investment in technology research helps businesses operate more efficiently. According to economist Lester Thurow, more than half of the productivity growth in the economy each year results from advances in technology.[23]

Kung Fu and Piano Wires: The Rules of Our Economy

In describing free-market economic systems, economist Ha-Joon Chang recalls the kung fu movies he watched as a child and his later shock when he learned that many of the stunts were made possible because the actors were suspended with piano wires. Like the invisible piano wires of these kung fu movies, our economy is made possible by a host of unseen rules and protections.[24] The fact that we take them for granted enables us to live the illusion that the economy is simply a natural occurrence—a miraculous organic ecosystem that functions best when left alone. It is not. Our economic system is made possible only because of copyright protections, private-property laws, courts for resolving disputes, and the predictability made possible through regulatory agencies like the SEC, the Federal Communications Commission (FCC), and others.

Over several centuries our society has created a framework of property law that gives particularly strong protection to private property. This framework enables individuals to own and sell many different types of property, using mechanisms such as real estate titles and stock ownership structures. Much wealth is now based on intellectual property—ideas, portals, and patents. The benefits of this protection for intellectual and physical property rights cannot be overestimated.

In an op-ed that appeared in *USA Today,* Abigail Disney (profiled in this book) writes about the loss of Walt and Roy Disney's first creation, Oswald the Lucky Rabbit, after the cartoon's distributor wrestled the rights away from them. She adds, "This loss was a huge setback for both men, and my grandfather vowed never to let himself be taken advantage of again. He soon registered a copyright on a new character named Mickey Mouse. It was 1928, and it was neither the first nor the last time the Walt Disney Co. benefited from a federal system of protections, laws and taxes that created fertile ground for building a business empire."[25]

Additionally, governmental regulations, including those that govern and stabilize financial markets, add tremendous value by providing stability and predictability to the environment. For Amy Domini (also profiled in this book), who started a mutual fund, the safety, order, and predictability of the market were central to her success. Similarly, in our profile of Jim Sherblom, he talks about the tremendous value that was added to Genzyme by going public. He estimates that the liquidity and the security provided by a regulated and fluid stock market accounts for 30 to 50 percent of a public company's value. We've also seen in 2008 what happens when those markets fail and the trust is broken. Sound financial regulation and transparency are essential to a functioning economy.

Public Investment in Individual Opportunity and a Strong Middle Class

Many economists have argued that when prosperity is broadly shared and the middle class is strong, as it was in the post-WWII era, economic growth is most robust.[26] Garrett Gruener, venture capitalist and founder of Ask.com, echoed this theme in a *Los Angeles Times* column:

> When inequality gets too far out of balance, as it did over the course of the last decade, the wealthy end up saving too much while members of the middle class can't afford to spend much unless they borrow excessively. Eventually, the economy stalls for lack of demand . . .
>
> What American businesspeople know, and have known since Henry Ford insisted that his employees be able to afford to buy the cars they made, is that a thriving economy doesn't just need investors; it needs people who can buy the goods and services businesses create. For the overall economy to do well, everyday Americans have to do well.[27]

At various points in US history, we've chosen to invest in individual opportunity in many ways. For more than a century, we've had a national commitment to public education for all citizens. We've also made tuition assistance available for higher education. The GI Bill, for example, was among the most successful wealth-broadening initiatives in US history.

We have also invested in other programs designed to broaden wealth, such as mortgage assistance for first-time homebuyers and flexible financing for business startups. Post–World War II housing programs were very successful at increasing opportunity and membership of the middle class, but due to racial and gender discrimination these initiatives were not universally available.

In addition to benefiting personally from these investments, many of the business leaders we've spoken to have also noted the benefit these investments played in building a strong middle class that can buy the products they sell, as articulated by Garrett Gruener in the quote above as well as by Jean Gordon of Frostyaire, who is quoted in the introduction.

Charitable and Civic Institutions

With the help of our tax system, which encourages charitable giving, we as a society have built an enviable infrastructure of charitable and cultural institutions. These include universities, hospitals, research institutes, humanitarian organizations, museums, and other cultural institutions. A number of the individuals we profile describe how they have benefited from private charities providing educational scholarships and research grants.

Colleagues and Employees

For anyone engaged in a large endeavor to state "I did it alone" renders invisible all the contributions of co-workers and colleagues, not to mention those who went before them in any given field. Ideas, products, and books do not emerge in a vacuum. Other people's creativity, labor, feedback, and suggestions are always involved. As President Franklin D. Roosevelt remarked, "Wealth in the modern world resulted from a combination of individual efforts. In spite of the great importance in our national life of the . . . ingenuity of unusual individuals, the people in the mass have inevitably helped to make large fortunes possible."[28]

Unfortunately, the contribution of the team, the helper, the editor, and the laborer are often undervalued in measuring wealth and achievement. Albert Einstein understood this: "A hundred times every day I tell myself that my inner and outer life are based on the labors of other men, living and dead, and that I must exert myself in order to give in the same measure as I have received and am still receiving."[29]

Like Einstein, many of the individuals profiled in this report talk about how they received tremendous support from colleagues. Ben Cohen, for example, believes that his employees were critical to Ben & Jerry's' profits and thus to his own success. His sentiments are echoed by Gun Denhart of Hanna Andersson clothing company; and Kim Jordan, CEO and co-founder of New Belgium Brewing, has much the same assessment.

CHAPTER 4

Stories of Success and the Common Good

About the Profiles

What follows is a series of profiles of business leaders—owners, founders, CEOs, and entrepreneurs—who tell the story of the built-together reality. Some of the business leaders profiled herein are people who have worked with the authors for many years through the Responsible Wealth project and United for a Fair Economy. Others are new to us. But in each of their stories is a recognition that their success is not entirely their own. Certainly hard work and creativity played a big part in nearly all these success stories, but so did luck, timing, a wide array of public investments, and an economic framework built through governmental action.

When we interviewed them for this book, we looked beyond questions about their personal characteristics and upbringing typical of many success biographies. Though the questions of modern success biographies have changed with the times, they still focus heavily on character and upbringing as they did in the nineteenth century. As historian Irvin Wyllie noted of these earlier biographies, "many of their questions were routine, but many were prejudicial."

> Was your boyhood spent in the country, or in a city? Did you work as a boy? Did you use tobacco previous to the age of 16?

Are you a church member? Is honesty necessary to business success? Should a country boy go to the big city if chances of success are fair in his own community? To what do you attribute your success? What maxims or watchwords have had a strong influence on your life and helped you to success? What books would you recommend to an ambitious boy?[1]

A modern biographer may substitute illegal drugs for tobacco, but the questions otherwise would be much the same. These questions obviously steer a subject to respond from a framework of individual character. That tradition of focusing on the personal traits while ignoring the contributions of society is a pervasive problem with the success stories told in our culture.

But what if we asked questions that went beyond individual character such as:

- What was the role of luck and timing in your success?

- Were you born White? Male? Tall? How might that have shaped your prospects?

- Were you educated in public schools and universities? Were your parents? What about your employees?

- Did you or your parents get direct government subsidies for higher education, homeownership, or business development? Did you benefit from other government programs?

- Did you inherit wealth or opportunities from your family?

- How did you or your business benefit directly or indirectly from public investment and taxpayer dollars or preferential tax treatment?

- What do you believe are your obligations to this society? What are your views toward taxation?

It was in this spirit that we approached the subjects of the profiles that follow. Most of the profiles are based on original interviews with the subjects in 2011, some of whom were also interviewed in 2003 or 2004 as part of an earlier report. We also included two profiles in this section that are drawn from public records.

We believe that these profiles, taken together, lay the foundation for a more nuanced narrative—the built-together reality—that recognizes successful businesspeople as more than islands floating in a void. Instead it views individuals as acting within an environment rich with public infrastructure built through generations of investment in the common good. The built-together reality credits good ideas and hard work but also points to the roles of timing, other individuals, society, and, importantly, government in supporting business success in this country. As such, the built-together reality leads to the public investment imperative—the idea that all of us, and especially the most successful and financially well off, need to contribute to the support of government to ensure that those public investments continue to be made.

Jerry Fiddler: Public Support for Education Helped Get Me Where I Am

Jerry Fiddler was co-founder, CEO, and chairman of Wind River Systems in Alameda, California. Now a mentor, an investor, and a professor of entrepreneurship, he helps entrepreneurs start new businesses.[2]

Unless you happen to be a computer programmer, you probably don't spend much time thinking about how a global positioning system (GPS) or a digital camera works or where the Mars rovers get their intelligence. All those devices have something in common: they're driven by software developed by a company you've probably never heard of—Wind River Systems. Based in Alameda, California, Wind River is a company born in part from government investment in research.

At the helm of Wind River for 26 years—first as founder and CEO and then as chairman—Jerry Fiddler knows that his success depended on many things, including public support of education, other people's investment, US government support of the Lawrence Berkeley Laboratory, and a whole lot of happenstance. In fact, were it not for a few quirks of fate, he might be a jazz musician, a photographer, or a geologist today.

Wind River Systems was sold to Intel in 2009 for $884 million. Fidder's share was more than $40 million. Now Fiddler "helps people start companies" as an investor in and consultant to start-ups in Silicon Valley, as an adjunct professor of entrepreneurship at the University of California at Berkeley, and as guest lecturer and mentor at Stanford University.

Education played an important role in Fiddler's success. After attending public school in Chicago, he went on to attend the University of Illinois, a land-grant college, where he majored in music and photography.

> I was the first person in my family to get a college degree. I went on and got a master's in computer science. I got out and got a job working at Lawrence Berkeley Laboratory as a computer scientist. I was making what seemed to me, at the time, to be an infinite amount of money. But I wanted something different. I wanted to affect the world in a different way. And I decided to start my own little consulting business.
>
> I called my dad, my parents, to tell them, and I was sure they were going to try to talk me out of it because here I was kind of living the dream—I had a stable job, responsible interesting work, prestigious—and I decided I was going to start my own business. I was 29 at the time. And my dad said, "Well it's about damn time." It was completely the opposite of what I expected to hear.

In addition to the importance of schooling, Fiddler acknowledges that his entrepreneurship has partially been the result of his upbringing. For him the two seem to go hand in hand: having the opportunity to attend school coupled with the support of family in his endeavors helped lead to his ability to set Wind River in

motion. A product of European thinking brought up in America,
Fiddler says,

> Being in a family situation that supported me to develop, and in
> schools with teachers who also helped me to learn and develop
> . . . you just don't do it on your own. You do it with the help
> of parents and friends and teachers and co-workers and service
> providers.
>
> My parents were both born here, but all four of my grandparents
> came from various parts of eastern Europe. My dad had busi-
> nesses: he had a fabric store, a lingerie shop, and that was just
> the way those folks thought about things; you don't work for
> somebody else. The way you grow up and become a real adult or
> *mensch* is you start a business, you run a business.
>
> And I think that's still happening, there's still that immigrant
> population that to a disproportionate degree really pushes entre-
> preneurship. And that population of course relies very heavily
> on what the public makes available to them, including public
> education. In turn those new businesses are a crucial driver of
> our economy.

Fiddler started Wind River Systems as a consulting company
in 1978 with his business partner, Dave Wilner, saying, "I don't
think I could have done it without him." As they moved from
consulting job to job, they built pieces of software for their own
repeated use; by 1987 Wind River had become a product-based
company, focused on selling that reusable software. The company
grew very quickly, more than doubling in size each year for six
consecutive years and going public in 1993.

Wind River's software is now found inside everything from
digital cameras, to cars and spacecraft, to the routers and the hubs
that control the Internet. From a few cutting-edge ideas, Fiddler
built a company that provides a critical piece of our technological infrastructure. At its peak in 2000, Wind River had 2,200
employees and was valued at $4 billion.

One of the things people don't talk about is how much we really rely on government institutions to maintain a fair playing field.

— Jerry Fiddler

Fiddler attributes his success to a combination of factors. "It's a wide variety of abilities and a willingness to take risks, coupled with a fair amount of luck." His ideas about luck have been informed by his varied life experiences:

> Something I learned as a musician is that being good is only one of many things you need to be successful. There are a million fabulous musicians out there who are never going to be successful because they don't have the other skills or support they need. They don't have the finance, the promotional backing, or the luck.

> And business is the same. There are millions of people who have the qualities that make you successful in business but who weren't lucky enough to be in the right place at the right time or to get the right help. So having the capabilities is necessary but nowhere near sufficient.

To Fiddler a big part of starting a successful business in the United States is the existence of a massive accounting, finance, and legal infrastructure to help companies get started and an education infrastructure to provide the needed skills.

> You can have a great idea in most countries in the world, but you won't be able to find the right advice, or the right accountants and lawyers, and you won't be able to get it financed. So, part of it is just being in a place where the opportunity exists to start a business. The angel and venture capital community and all the support structure around it is massive and unique; it really doesn't exist in the same way anywhere else in the world.

> There's no way I would be here if I hadn't worked at a national lab. It was the best place in the world to learn how to do this. I probably wouldn't have gotten that job if I hadn't had a master's degree, which I got from a public university. I wouldn't have had that master's or a bachelor's degree if there weren't financial aid and an assistantship in grad school. And had I not gone to a good public school, I probably wouldn't have gotten *into* the university. So you just keep stepping back. Heck, if my mother hadn't had the right prenatal care, I could have been 28 IQ points less intelligent! So where does it start?

Fiddler reflects on how his personal success has been affected by the right circumstances in his life, but he also points to the importance of well-functioning business and financial sectors. The economy functions with rules and regulations that ultimately benefit entrepreneurs and businesspeople. Fiddler believes that many are slow to recognize government's important role:

> One of the things people don't talk about is how much we really rely on government institutions to maintain a fair playing field. Entrepreneurship is an equalizer, a way that people who aren't wealthy can become more wealthy, can become more independent, and in the process can provide a huge amount of benefit to society as a whole. But we live in a society right now that is going in exactly the opposite direction. The disparity in wealth between the bottom and the top is growing dramatically, and the middle class is being squeezed out.

All of us, but especially entrepreneurs, rely on the government's role of creating a level playing field, and people like the SEC and the FTC [Federal Trade Commission] and other regulating agencies are critical to entrepreneurship. Large business interests obviously put huge effort into lobbying, much of it into reducing regulation, but for small businesses, for startups, that regulation is important. The only way that you can have a healthy startup economy is if you have a level playing field that allows those companies to come into being and to compete, and that has to come back to some level of regulation; the government has to be regulating.

Noting the interdependent nature of our economic system, Fiddler continues, pointing out some of the things that most people take for granted:

And then there's the rest of the infrastructure that we need—the roads and the railroads, transportation and information infrastructure that makes wealth creation possible in this country.

To take it up to a higher level, as a country we are absolutely the envy of the world in terms of the intellectual horsepower we put together—the creativity, the technology, the leadership. Why is that here? To me much of it is a product of the entrepreneurial system and of the immigrants who prized education, learning, and initiative. But most of all, it's a product of the public education system.

Fiddler is quick to highlight the ways in which he did not create his success purely on his own. From a supportive family with entrepreneurial spirit, Fiddler had the opportunity to pursue higher education and then to begin his own business. As an entrepreneur he's not afraid to say that he has benefited from governmental regulation. Fiddler is also not afraid to admit that he has been lucky: "It all builds. In this country there is more opportunity and mobility than anywhere else in the world. But it's very rare that a lot of factors beyond the individual haven't contributed, a lot of stars haven't aligned properly to create someone's success."

Glynn Lloyd: Transportation and Food Safety Regulations Help My Business

Glynn Lloyd is the founder of City Fresh Foods, a Boston-based food service and delivery company.[3]

The importance of hard work and a reliable team of advisers is not lost on City Fresh Foods founder Glynn Lloyd. He has taken the lead role from the start but gives credit to his brother Sheldon as well as the people he has relied on over the years, from employees to consultants, for helping to make his business successful.

Lloyd, a leader in the Boston African-American business community, started the business in 1994 with the help of a $20,000 loan from the City of Boston's Department of Neighborhood Development (DND) to help him build out his first kitchen on Dudley Street. This loan was the money that helped launch the business. By 1998 City Fresh Foods outgrew its Dudley Street kitchen, and the City of Boston helped the company relocate to a vacant foreclosed building that it was able to purchase in nearby Dorchester.

In 2009 City Fresh Foods took on a $400,000 investment in renovating its current 14,000-square-foot building in Boston's Roxbury neighborhood, which now serves as its headquarters and production facility. Even with 15 years of success and nearly $5 million in sales, City Fresh Foods' margins were so slim that it took investments from the DND and the state's Economic Stabilization Trust as well as a $100,000 equipment lease to make the project work.

Lloyd has worked hard and taken some leaps of faith to make City Fresh Foods what it is today—a company that in 2011 had 80 employees and $7 million in sales—but he is quick to credit the many employees who make the place tick. He also recognizes the role that the public education system plays in making his business possible: "The folks here are mostly all educated through the public school system. The fact that they can read and write and use a computer and all that stuff is pretty important to us. You know, a certain level of education coming in is important."

A product of the Sharon, Massachusetts, public schools, Lloyd got his start as an entrepreneur back in fourth grade, when he started cutting lawns in his Sharon neighborhood. He soon realized that he could pay other kids $4 or $5 per hour to do the lawn-mowing jobs that earned him $10. By high school he had a landscaping company with two trucks and a team of employees; he was hooked. "I had a knack for numbers and I loved people, so the combination of all those things worked for me."

Lloyd sees himself as a motivator, capable of bringing out the best in others and of "creating order from chaos." Where others saw a burned-out building, Lloyd pictured a thriving renovated warehouse with well-trained staff preparing tasty, nutritious, affordable meals and delivering them all around the Boston metro area; he motivated everyone around him to make his dream a reality.

City Fresh Foods operates in what Lloyd refers to as the "public market," meaning the majority of its contracts are for public school meals and publicly subsidized meals for seniors. While those contracts account for much of the company's income, it's in the indirect government investments where it becomes evident how every small business—in fact, every business of any size—relies heavily on public structures.

> Well, let's talk about transportation. We're a delivery company. We're going 60 to 70 miles north, east, and south. So without roads, we have no business. We're using backroads, side roads, and highways. Interesting enough, this was a tough year for us because we do a lot of the schools. Due to the heavy snow, we lost five days of school this year in terms of business, which is unheard of in the past few years. But there would have been a lot more if we didn't have the infrastructure to clean the streets [and] put the salt down, which I know is very expensive, actually.

Lloyd also talks about the importance of public transportation for his employees to get to work. Though some walk or drive, he notes that many of his employees rely on Boston's public transit system, including many employees who moved with the company from its Dudley Street location to its current Shirley Street location, about 3 miles away. From a business point of view, urban mass transit systems help expand the pool of employees that companies can draw from in looking for staff to fill their work needs. The state's investment in the Massachusetts Bay Transportation Authority, including its trains, subways, and extensive bus routes, is a significant benefit to businesses of all sizes that is often taken for granted.

More than most companies, City Fresh Foods relies on natural gas to cook its products and electricity to power its operations; and like many businesses, the company is "completely computer-reliant, Internet reliant," although Lloyd admits he rarely thinks about those things. Warren Buffett and Bill Gates Sr. talk about what would happen, or rather what wouldn't happen, if you plunked an entrepreneur down in the middle of a developing country. Lloyd had a taste of that recently, when the Boston water supply was shut down for a number of days:

> Water . . . clean water. We had the issue this year where there was a little concern around water contamination, and they shut it down. We had to pull our water from a different reservoir. And we had to literally boil all of our water here, and it took us back in time. I mean, you talk about taking for granted. I was saying, "What happens if you didn't have water?" Well, we experienced it this past year. So, those are the basics. We treat it like the air that we breathe, but the reality is, without it, you're out of business.

Providing health care to employees is one of the most difficult aspects of owning a small business. Massachusetts law now requires that all citizens be insured. City Fresh Foods already pays more than most employers in the food preparation business. It pays half of its employees' health-care premiums for individuals and one-third for employees with families. "It gets expensive for

PHOTO COURTESY OF GLYNN LLOYD

It's funny, because typically as an entrepreneur, you're not asking for more regulation, but clearly it's a benefit because people know their food is safe.

— GLYNN LLOYD *(left, with his brother Sheldon)*

employees to cover those health costs, the chunk that they have to support." But Lloyd estimates that half of his employees are using the low-cost MassHealth plan.

Unemployment insurance as well is very helpful to City Fresh Foods and its employees. Lloyd continues, "On very few occasions, we have had to lay off people here, and during the summer . . . due to some of our contracts' seasonality, we have laid employees off for the summer. And I know that's a lifeline for the folks whom we've had to lay off, so there has been a direct benefit to folks."

And in the food business, Lloyd is well aware that City Fresh Foods relies on food inspections and certifications, both

coming in the door and going out: "With qualified vendors coming in, we need to know that they're handling product correctly,
so "USDA Inspected" is one of those things that we look for in
terms of our supply side. That's federal, and then you have your
state and your local inspection services, which actually are a stamp
of approval to *our* customers because they know that we're abid-
ing by basic healthy sanitation practices of how we're handling
our products here."

These safety standards are not creations of an invisible hand.
They are the result of a public outcry and governmental action following the muckraking journalism—including Upton Sinclair's
The Jungle—that exposed unsanitary and unhealthy practices. At
the federal level, Congress passed both the Meat Inspection Act
and the Food and Drug Act in 1906 to ensure that public health
was not compromised.[4] Both laws have since been expanded and
updated as the industries have changed, ensuring the safety of our
food supply for more than 100 years.

"It's funny," says Lloyd, "because typically as an entrepreneur
you're not asking for more regulation, but . . . clearly it's a benefit
because people know their food is safe. And, listen, if we have to
do it, we want to make sure our competitors are doing it, and overall it's trying to protect the health and the safety of our population,
our kids."

Food safety inspections, from the farm to the table, provide
public confidence that is essential to any successful food service
business.

Lloyd is hopeful that standards for what is served in schools
will be changing for the better—away from fats, sugars, and empty
calories and toward "real foods," including leaner meats and
unprocessed vegetables. He's been pushing the city toward reallo-
cating some of its 800 acres of vacant land toward urban agriculture. Both of these changes would help Lloyd and City Fresh Foods
do their job even better.

Highways and Transportation

From the earliest days of our nation's history, there has been a clear public role in creating and maintaining a transportation system that connects the nation and promotes the common good. President George Washington's first address to the new Congress in 1790 called for "the advancement of agriculture, commerce, and manufactures by all proper means"[5] and "facilitating the intercourse between the distant parts of the country by due attention to the post-office and post-roads [roads designated for transporting mail]."[6] Thus the government began linking the nation with roads, ports, railroads, and post offices and investing large amounts of capital for the cause, including "approximately 70 percent of the capital for the construction of canals and 30 percent for railroads."[7]

Later, through a series of massive land grants and public subsidies, a system of railroads was built to connect the nation's disparate communities and urban centers. The most notable of that era was the Pacific Railway Act of 1862 that granted more than 115 million acres of public land and $60 million in loans to create the nation's first transcontinental railroad, giving birth to the Union Pacific and Central Pacific Railroad companies in the process.[8]

The government's role in advancing and funding national transportation remained central throughout the twentieth century. While early discussion of a national system of "superhighways" began under President Franklin Roosevelt in the 1930s,[9] it finally came to fruition under President Dwight Eisenhower with the Federal-Aid Highway Act of 1956. Similar to other Cold War investments with national defense as one of the motivating factors, the new Interstate Highway System allowed the United States to move troops and equipment across the country rapidly. Nevertheless the fringe benefits to society as a whole were huge.

Over the coming years, an entirely new system of limited-access highways was built from the ground up at a cost of nearly $130 billion,

$114 billion of which was federal funds.[10] Although this government investment created thousands of jobs in the process of construction, it also resulted in a significant increase in economic activity over the long term by reducing production and shipping costs and making inexpensive land more accessible.[11]

While it's rare to hear a business owner refer to it explicitly, most US businesses benefit significantly from our publicly funded transportation infrastructure. In her *USA Today* column published in August 2010, Abigail Disney (profiled in this book) noted, "The transportation and federal highway system built in the wake of World War II took millions of visitors to Disneyland,"[12] helping build her family's wealth.

Responsible Wealth member Judy Pigott notes of her family's wealth, "the [Peterbilt and Kenworth] trucks PACCAR manufactures would have nowhere to travel without the roadways, highways, bridges, and tunnels that the government builds and maintains."[13]

The beneficial relationship extends to other forms of transit as well. Amy Domini, CEO of Domini Social Investments (also profiled in this book), recognizes the importance of the New York City subway system, joking that "all subways lead to SoHo,"[14] where her offices are located.

Another Responsible Wealth member, John Russell from Portland, Oregon, acknowledges the financial benefits his real estate venture received due to the extensive public transportation options around his commercial properties: "Without investments by the City of Portland, the state of Oregon, and the federal government in redeveloping downtown Portland—particularly the investments in light rail and streetcar systems—my success would not have been possible."[15]

In 2009 the American Recovery and Reinvestment Act (ARRA) allocated significant new funds to build on this long history by investing in the next generation of transportation infrastructure, including both high-speed rail and mass transit. The Department of Transportation was granted $45.5 billion for new transport systems,[16] of which $10 billion[17] is allocated for high-speed-rail development projects, moving toward a more sustainable mode of public transportation.

Thelma Kidd: Taxes Are Just the Price of Doing Business

Thelma Kidd is the co-founder of Davis-Kidd Booksellers, which grew to four stores across Tennessee, employing more than 200 people before being sold to another independent bookseller in 1997.[18]

Thelma Kidd grew up in the West Texas town of Slaton, just outside Lubbock, a dry and dusty part of Texas where rainfall averages only 21 inches per year.[19] Her first exposure to entrepreneurship came through her father. "My father was a building contractor," she says. "He was definitely an entrepreneur, although I wouldn't have known that word then. He started working for himself very early on, and his philosophy and belief about money—that there is not a paycheck that comes in regularly and that there wasn't one particular company he worked for—prepared me for being a business owner. Working for myself, that's really what fits for me—doing my own thing."

Kidd got her formal education in the public school system of Slaton before going on to study briefly at a private college; she then finished her undergraduate degree at Texas Tech University in Lubbock, a public university. She received her graduate degree in social work from the University of Michigan, Ann Arbor, another public university, after which she worked for a few years as a therapist.

It was while working as a therapist in Ann Arbor that she saw a new kind of bookstore—the original Borders Books. Later she moved to Tennessee, where she joined with her college friend, Karen Davis, to explore the idea of starting such a bookstore in Nashville. Kidd's love for bookstores, more than the idea of "starting a business," motivated her. Specifically, she wanted to create a bookstore that honored free thought and differing opinions: "I liked the idea of having a magazine rack where two people could be standing side by side, and one could be reading the *Buddhist Review* and the other *Christianity Today*, and those people would both be welcome in the store. To me that is progress."

Meanwhile, in Washington, DC, big changes were under way that would have a major impact on Kidd and Davis's business plans. Julie Weeks of the National Women's Business Council writes of the events that led up to President Jimmy Carter's signing of Executive Order 12138:

> Women have started, owned and inherited businesses in the United States since the founding of the country, yet official recognition and support for women's enterprise development has been in existence only for the past 25 years . . .
>
> The first federal government program to assist women's business enterprises came as the direct result of lobbying from women business owners. Due to their efforts not only in lobbying the federal government but in urging the appointment of women in key agency positions, an interagency government task force was created, and a research study was conducted to review the status of women-owned firms in the US. The resulting report, "The Bottom Line: Unequal Enterprise in America," documented some of the barriers that women faced in starting and growing their businesses. In response to the report, President Jimmy Carter issued an executive order in 1979 establishing an Office of Women's Business Ownership within the US Small Business Administration.
>
> Shortly thereafter, a pilot loan program was established, the office began working with federal procurement officials to get more women-owned businesses involved in selling goods and services to the government, and began reaching out to the women's business community through speeches, conferences, and news releases.[20]

It was in 1979, the same year the executive order was signed and a year before their business formally opened, that Kidd and Davis received one of these new Small Business Administration (SBA) loans for women entrepreneurs. They scraped together about $50,000 of their own, mostly borrowed from relatives, which was matched by a $175,000 SBA-guaranteed loan. Kidd

PHOTO BY CHRIS DAVIS

I agree with something one of my mentors said:
"I want to pay a lot of taxes, because that would
mean I'm making a lot of money." It is fair.

— THELMA KIDD *(left, with her daughter and granddaughter)*

notes, "It was a bank loan; but the SBA guaranteed if we defaulted that the bank would get 90 percent of their funding back from the SBA." This guarantee helped Kidd and Davis overcome some of the major hurdles they faced as women starting a business.

"It was challenging being women going into business because there was a lot of resistance from Realtors," says Kidd, "and we weren't taken as seriously as I think we would have been had we been male. On the other hand, there was this funding available that was to encourage women to go into business, and that helped; that really was a great boost. I don't know that we could have done it without that."

Expanding on the challenges of being taken seriously as women entrepreneurs when approaching banks, Kidd adds, "We would have stunned looks or blank stares that would come back at us when we talked about what we were planning to do. The bankers and Realtors assumed that we were not serious about it, that we would get tired of it after six months and quit. I don't think they assume that about a man who walks in."

Thanks in part to the SBA-guaranteed loan, they overcame these challenges and opened their first store in the Green Hills neighborhood of Nashville in 1980. It was busy from the very beginning, which Kidd attributes to great timing and a bookstore model that was new to Nashville. Instead of the typical small bookstore with 2,500 titles, the new Davis-Kidd Booksellers had closer to 25,000 titles in their large, 3,500-square-foot store. Later they moved and expanded again to 9,000 square feet. The store eventually grew to 25,000 square feet and more than 100,000 titles.

They also tried other new strategies, such as staying open at night and seven days a week. This was pushing the boundaries far out for a Nashville bookstore in 1980, but it paid off. Within a few years, they opened up additional stores in Memphis (1985), Knoxville (1986), and Jackson (1995). When they finally sold the company to another independent bookseller in 1997, they had more than 200 employees and four stores, three of which included cafés.

Kidd acknowledges the importance of timing and luck, in addition to hard work, saying, "Things turn in your favor periodically, and it's not just because you're a good person or you worked hard, because things go against you sometimes, too, and it's not because you are a bad person or you weren't working hard. I do think that people who are successful need to be really dedicated and committed and have vision. But that alone is not enough. You need things going your way periodically."

Kidd also talks about the importance of public investments and the stable regulatory environment in supporting her business. She acknowledges the role that public schools, libraries, and safe communities have played in her own life, but also talks of the benefits her stores received: "Obviously, when you have a retail store or any kind of public place, people are going to come in and use your space. I'm glad there were building inspectors and health inspectors for the café. It's like a third-party check on what we were doing. That we had access to those people with the knowledge to keep our facilities safe was actually helpful, and it protected us."

As Oliver Wendell Holmes once declared, "Taxes are the price we pay for civilization." Kidd's view on taxes is similar, noting that it's just the price of doing business:

> I don't remember feeling resentful of having to pay taxes or having to pay for all the various licenses that you have to pay for. I mean, it is a hassle, it is money, but it's business. It's part of the price of doing business . . .
>
> If your business doesn't generate enough for you to be paying the various things you're supposed to be paying, then your business model doesn't work. You know, you need to do something different. You need to adjust something. That just feels like energy that is so wasted, to be mad at the government . . .
>
> I agree with something one of my mentors said: "I want to pay a lot of taxes because that would mean I'm making a lot of money." It is fair.

Warren Buffett: This Society Disproportionately Values What I Do Well

Warren Buffett founded Berkshire Hathaway and lives in Omaha, Nebraska.

Warren Buffett, the founder of Berkshire Hathaway and the second-wealthiest man in the United States, is hailed as one of the most successful stock market investors ever.[21] Yet this does not prevent Buffett from acknowledging the role of the uniquely fertile soil of the American economic system in amassing his wealth. At a 1996 Berkshire Hathaway annual meeting, Buffett noted that the

US system "provides me with enormous rewards for what I bring to this society."[22]

Although we referenced the following quote in the introduction, it is worth repeating here. In a television interview, Buffett stated: "I personally think that society is responsible for a very significant percentage of what I've earned. If you stick me down in the middle of Bangladesh or Peru or someplace, you'll find out how much this talent is going to produce in the wrong kind of soil. I will be struggling 30 years later. I work in a market system that happens to reward what I do very well—disproportionately well."[23]

Buffett feels he is not only fortunate to have been born in the United States but also lucky that he "came wired at birth with a talent for capital allocation."[24] He bought his first stock when he was just 11 years old, from which he made a $5 profit. When his family moved to Washington, DC, from Omaha, Buffett had two paper routes, earning him $175 per month; he also had a business that made $200 per month from pinball machines and peanut vending machines.[25] After graduating from Woodrow Wilson High School, Buffett attended the University of Pennsylvania for two years before transferring to the University of Nebraska. He later earned his master's at Columbia Business School.[26]

Upon graduation Buffett worked as an investment salesman in Omaha for several years before taking a job at the Graham-Newman Corporation in New York. He returned to Omaha in 1957 and began Buffett Partnership Ltd. In 1962 his partnership bought shares in a textile-manufacturing firm called Berkshire Hathaway; he eventually took control in 1965 and used the company as a means to invest in others. Since then Berkshire Hathaway has acquired stock in such corporations as the Washington Post Company, ABC, Coca-Cola, and Gillette, and it even owns various companies, such as GEICO and FlightSafety.[27] His successful investing strategies, which follow a value investing philosophy, made Buffett a millionaire and eventually a billionaire. He is currently the chairman, CEO, and largest shareholder of Berkshire Hathaway.[28]

I think that people at the high end—people like myself—should be paying a lot more in taxes. We have it better than we've ever had it.

— WARREN BUFFETT

But Buffett recognizes that while his particular skills have been and continue to be highly valued in the marketplace, the skills of other people are undervalued:

> If you're a marvelous teacher, this world won't pay a lot for it. If you are a terrific nurse, this world will not pay a lot for it . . . I do think that when you're treated enormously well by this market system, where in effect the market system showers the ability to buy goods and services on you because of some peculiar talent—maybe your adenoids are a certain way, so you can sing and everybody will pay you enormous sums to be on television or whatever—I think society has a big claim on that.[29]

Consequently, Buffett's attitude toward society shapes his perspective on taxation. He has said, "If you're in the luckiest 1 percent of humanity, you owe it to the rest of humanity to think about the other 99 percent."[30] Thus, Buffett is a staunch advocate for progressive taxation to "partially redress" existing inequality.[31]

He pointed out that in 2011 his taxable income of around $46 million was taxed at only 17.4 percent, a fraction of what others pay.[32] He believes this is unfair. In a recent interview with ABC, he detailed his feelings: "If anything, taxes for the lower and middle class and maybe even the upper middle class should even probably be cut further. But I think that people at the high end—people like myself—should be paying a lot more in taxes. We have it better than we've ever had it."[33]

Buffett is also an advocate for the estate tax. In 2007 he testified before the Senate Finance Committee about its importance: "Dynastic wealth, the enemy of a meritocracy, is on the rise. Equality of opportunity has been on the decline. A progressive and meaningful estate tax is needed to curb the movement of a democracy toward plutocracy."[34]

In addition to supporting policy measures that address gross inequalities of our economic system, Buffett is a well-known philanthropist. In 2006 he announced that he would give away all of his Berkshire Hathaway stock to philanthropic foundations, with most of it going to the Bill and Melinda Gates Foundation. Then, in 2010, Buffett pledged to give away 99 percent of his wealth during his lifetime or at his death because, as he put it, "fate's distribution of long straws is wildly capricious."[35]

Martin Rothenberg: My Success Was Paid For by Others

Martin Rothenberg was founder and CEO of Syracuse Language Systems, based in Syracuse, New York.[36]

Martin Rothenberg forgets neither where he came from nor the help he received along the way. Now a successful entrepreneur in Upstate New York, Rothenberg is quick to credit the many public resources that were available to him.

Rothenberg's story begins in Brooklyn. The son of immigrant parents—a housepainter and a sales clerk—he attended public schools there. Says Rothenberg: "I started my movement to technology by going to the Electricity and Radio section of the local public library when I was maybe 12 or 13 years old. I picked out all the books on that subject, and I found one that I thought I could understand without any help. I just read it from cover to cover."

In a New York City technical high school, he took his first formal classes in technology. But money for college was not in the family budget: "If I went to college, I would have to pay for it myself. I could never take money from [my parents] for a college education—that wouldn't be fair. That would come from the savings they had for their retirement."

Following high school Rothenberg put his technical skills to use doing television repair, and he considered opening a shop of his own. But he was drafted into the army in 1953, and after Signal Corps training he spent 14 months in Korea. As the end of his tour of duty approached, Rothenberg recalls learning about what the GI Bill offered: "When I got home, they were offering me a full scholarship, including tuition and a stipend to live on. You'd have to be foolish to turn it down. By making it easy to attend college, the GI Bill encouraged people to make that step, to give up the immediate income for possible gains in their lifestyle and financial status later on. That's what it did for me."

After graduating from the University of Michigan in electrical engineering, Rothenberg took a job with Hughes Aircraft, then another in the space program at Bendix. His wife's degree program took him back to the University of Michigan, where he learned about a full fellowship for a new three-year graduate program that combined computers and language. He notes that the fellowship program was under the National Defense Education Act, a direct result of the Russians' launching the *Sputnik* satellite, as the country realized that there were not enough Americans educated in the area of technology. He was accepted into the program and had a necessary fourth year of graduate work funded by a loan, forgivable on the condition that he go into teaching.

The forgivable loan biased me somewhat toward going into education. I think that most people don't realize the extent to which the technology programs at the universities are sponsored by the government. Besides the sponsorship of my education, I had research grants all the way through my teaching career, starting from the first year. There were a couple of grants from private foundations, but mainly they were government grants.

Besides paying for part of my own salary and lab equipment, the grants included tuition and stipends for assistants. So the young people who work for you in your laboratory are mostly paid for by the government. My university research provided the basis for Syracuse Language Systems. So that's in large part where my wealth came from.

After graduate school, he went on to teach at Syracuse University for 25 years, from 1966 to 1991.

After the death of his wife in 1990, Rothenberg retired and started Syracuse Language Systems, which developed multimedia software for language learning. Of the company name, he says, "The reason I called it 'Syracuse' was because it was the Syracuse area that had all the skills necessary to make a high-tech software company. We had talented artists, programmers, marketing specialists, and linguists for the language software. And, of course, most of those people were educated in our public education system."

He started the business slowly, with just a few people, including his son, starting out in a government-sponsored "incubator" that provided below-market rent and subsidized support services.

I had the ability, which was given to me by my graduate studies, to understand what's right and wrong in speech patterns and, from my engineering experience, how to measure that and give corrective feedback to people. So I have those technical capabilities, which are not commonly found in one person. Usually, someone is either a linguist or an engineer, not both.

When I left the university in 1991, some people thought I, as an academic, could not do well in business. . . . They didn't know

By making it easy to attend college, the GI Bill encouraged people to make that step. That's what it did for me.

— Martin Rothenberg

my grandmother. My grandmother was an entrepreneur who was always in business even though she couldn't read or write English, at least not too well.

As a software developer, the company relied heavily on patent and copyright law to protect its products. Says Rothenberg:

> Intellectual property protection is important. You can't accumulate a lot of money or resources without someone stealing it from you, and a government has to protect you and stop that from happening. I have a number of patents. In my present company [Glottal Enterprises], for example, it would be easy for a larger company to reproduce what we are doing, except for the fact that I do have some patents protecting a lot of what I am doing now.
>
> Syracuse Language Systems was the first company to make a consumer product using computer-based speech recognition, and I was awarded a patent in that area that protected our innovation. At a financially crucial time, we were able to get a sizeable legal

settlement from one company that was copying our programs in Japan. On the other hand, one reason we couldn't go into China was because they *didn't* enforce copyright laws.

Not only was Rothenberg able to rely on the US government to protect his product but he also gives credit to the government for starting the Internet. "In the last years of our ownership of the company, we were heavily invested in using the Internet for language instruction."

That's not to say that the government couldn't do more to support small businesses and level the playing field. Rothenberg reflects on some of the challenges faced by small businesses in America: "For example, one problem in hiring [at] a small company is health care. It is hard for us to pay for health care. Government health care, at least minimum health care, would make that better for us."

In addition to his technical and linguistic skills, Rothenberg sees his strength as an entrepreneur as setting a clear vision for the company that everyone understands, motivating people, knowing his own limitations, and bringing in the right people to help him. But he's quick to point out that he didn't—in fact, he couldn't—do it alone:

> You can't have a company doing especially high-tech work without a network of people that you can draw on—skills that you can draw on—for technical management [and] marketing skills. There is nothing that I could have done alone. My father was a house painter; all he needed was the paint and he would get paid for painting somebody's house. But you can't build a high-tech company by yourself in that way.
>
> The first thing that you have to do is gather a team. There's not much you can do as one person. You could start a small retail business, like my daughter has, but you're not going to make a *lot* of wealth that way. Generally, you have a team.

Unless you can find 76 hours in your workday, you just can't do everything yourself.

When Rothenberg and his financial partners eventually sold Syracuse Language Systems in 1998, it was worth approximately $30 million. With a part of his portion of the proceeds, he established a small family charitable foundation dedicated to children, education, and the environment.

He does not forget the people who made his success possible. Together with most of the other stockholders, Rothenberg gave a parting bonus to the company's long-term employees. He adds, "I consider grants from the charitable foundation to be in some measure from all the personnel of my former company, with my family acting as trustees."

R E A L I T Y   C H E C K

Higher Education and Individual Success

There is little doubt that education is an essential ingredient for success in today's economy. All of the entrepreneurs and business leaders in this book are college graduates, and most received their educations through our public university system. The vast majority also attended public schools prior to their college careers.

Although there were several colonial colleges like Yale, Harvard, and Princeton in the nation's early years, they focused on educating a small number of elites.[37] By the mid-1800s, as the economy underwent a radical transformation, a new kind of university was required. Congress responded by passing the Morrill Acts of 1862 and 1890 that dramatically expanded the availability of higher education across the nation. These acts granted up to 1 million acres of public lands in each state to be developed for use as public colleges and universities.[38] More than 105 colleges and university systems in the United States and its territories have been created as a result of the Morrill Acts.[39]

As World War II ended, another expansion of educational opportunity took place in the United States. Passed in 1944, the GI Bill enabled many veterans who often did not have the means to pursue education to enroll in school, resulting in a surge of student enrollment.[40] The bill's success led to legislation in 1952 and 1966 establishing similar programs for veterans of the Korean and Vietnam Wars as well as those who served in peacetime. Martin Rothenberg is one of the beneficiaries of the GI Bill.

In 1965 the Pell Grant program was created to provide direct financial assistance for low- and middle-income students who wanted to attend college. Many individuals profiled in this book, including Kim Jordan of New Belgium Brewing (profiled next), as well as one of the authors of this book, received Pell Grants. Both the Pell Grant program and the various veteran programs supplemented an education system that also received substantial taxpayer support, as the broad societal benefits gained by expanding educational opportunity were widely recognized at the time.

In recent years there has been a significant backslide in public funding for higher education. To make up for the losses in governmental funding, public colleges have raised tuition costs. From 2000 to 2010, public four-year institutions increased tuition and fees at a rate averaging 5.6 percent.[41] Higher education has faced even greater challenges amid the Great Recession. For the 2009–2010 academic year, tuition hikes hovered around 10 percent for public universities.[42] In 2009 state appropriations for higher education dropped by a stunning 9 percent.[43] This would have been a double-digit drop without the $4 billion provided under the American Recovery and Reinvestment Act.[44]

As a result of the rising costs of college, students are increasingly relying on financial aid to pay for their education. Pell Grants have not, however, kept pace with the cost of attendance. The average Pell Grant in 2007 was $2,737, less than the 1976 average of $2,862 (both in 2009 dollars).[45] As part of the economic recovery efforts, ARRA included a dramatic increase in Pell Grant funding that expanded both the average grant amount to $3,646—an increase of 40 percent from 2007[46]—and the number of recipients.[47] Nevertheless the maximum total Pell Grant award in 1979 covered about 75 percent of the total cost of attending a four-year college; in 2011 the maximum award covered just about one-third.[48]

Higher tuition costs and inadequate Pell Grants have fueled an increase in student loans: 35 percent of undergraduates took out Stafford loans in 2009–2010, up from 23 percent 10 years earlier. They also took out more money on average.[49] Saddling a generation of graduates with debt has a stifling effect on entrepreneurship in the United States. Instead of taking a chance at starting a new business, they are compelled to take the first job that comes along to ensure that they can make their loan payments.

Kim Jordan: The Idea of a Self-Made Person Is a Stretch

Kim Jordan is a co-founder and the CEO of New Belgium
Brewing, the nation's third-largest craft brewer.[50]

Established in 1991, New Belgium Brewing is the maker of the popular Fat Tire beer, among many others.[51] Since its founding, the Fort Collins, Colorado–based company has grown rapidly. It is now the third-largest craft brewer in the nation,[52] with more than 400 employees, including 250 in Colorado and another 150 across the nation. At the company's helm is CEO and co-founder Kim Jordan.

Jordan makes clear her view of the self-made myth: "This whole notion of the self-made person is a stretch. . . . If you live in a farm community, which I have done, you see that neighbors are wildly dependent on one another: 'I'll come help you put up your hay; you'll plow my road.' It is certainly more of a myth than a reality, and that's just the interpersonal part. You know, one neighbor to another."

Expanding her example to the role of government, Jordan adds:

Then you have the whole, "Well, wait a minute. How about all of the subsidies for farming, or the county road system, or the fact that school buses drive long, long ways out of the way to pick kids up to be able to attend public school?" You know, it seems like the purpose of the government is to be able to fund things that we can't fund . . . by ourselves because it's just too expensive to do.

So [the myth] has a lot of romance to it, I guess. Although I'm not quite sure why we feel compelled to say that we don't need to rely on one another.

Jordan speaks highly of the public investments, coordinated through the Downtown Development Authority (DDA) that have revitalized downtown Fort Collins, where New Belgium Brewing is based: "The quality of life in downtown Fort Collins is much improved because we have a Development Authority that's able to use tax increment financing to make really cool projects downtown that are vastly improving the cultural vibe of the community."

Small and large cities across the United States have such a development authority that works to "foster economic, cultural, and social growth"[53] in their downtown areas. In 2010 the Fort Collins DDA renovated two alleys, stringing up lights, planting flowers in pots, and utilizing quarried boulders as benches. The DDA has also helped fund the improvement of more than 70 facades in Fort Collins, simultaneously promoting "green building practices and projects," which the 2010 DDA Annual Report says attract green businesses that are more likely to fund community projects.[54]

Jordan reflects on the many public investments made possible through our tax system that have helped New Belgium succeed: "Beer is heavy, and it needs to be transported in vehicles. Certainly the public highway system, the federal system, has been hugely

Beer is heavy,
and it needs to
be transported in
vehicles. Certainly
the public highway
system . . . has been
hugely important
to New Belgium
Brewing.

— KIM JORDAN

PHOTO BY CRAIG DEMARTINO

important to [New Belgium Brewing]. . . . We are in an enterprise zone, and so the credits we receive for that, both in hiring and in investments have been important. The tax credits for purchasing equipment have been really helpful to us, and we probably would not have been able to grow as we have without those because there were years when they were pretty significant."

In the crucial early years of the operation, New Belgium received a $40,000 Small Business Administration loan. "We were probably three years into it [the business] . . . so at the time, that was pretty substantial." The company also benefited from services provided by the local land-grant university, Colorado State University (CSU), and a grant from the Department of Energy to encourage innovation and new energy technologies.

We work a lot with CSU in pilot programs where they want a
test facility for some project or another. So just the fact that we
have a land-grant university in our town is helpful to us, all the
way from microbiology through energy management. . . .

We are part of a test project, a grant through the Department
of Energy. . . . Being a part of that project, on the one hand it
compelled us—or rather forced us, I guess—to invest a few million dollars, but on the other hand we were able to get a couple
of million dollars out of the program as well for both hardware
and software for energy management and for renewable energy
production. So that was a benefit.

Like almost all business owners, Jordan took great risks in her
life. She and her then-husband took out a second mortgage on
their home, along with credit card debt, to raise the seed money
they needed to start the business. At one point she had to borrow
$5,000 from family to make payroll, but in the end she emerged a
very successful businesswoman.

Jordan acknowledges that she was also lucky on many levels.
Both of her parents were college graduates who were politically
active and engaged in the community. In addition to providing a
stable home environment, her parents could afford to send her to a
private Quaker school, where she learned some of the bedrock values she holds to this day and which have influenced the company
as well. Says Jordan: "George Fox, who was one of the founders
of the Quaker movement in the United States, has a quote, which
is, 'Let your life speak.' And in terms of the way that we operate
New Belgium, I think that's been really influential for me because I
think one of the things that you come to see as a successful entrepreneur is that you can use profits to do really interesting work."

Jordan benefited in many ways from the public structures in
our society. She completed her college degree at CSU, a land-grant
college as noted above. While she worked her way through college, she received publicly guaranteed student loans and a few Pell

Grants along the way. Jordan was also fortunate to have attended CSU at a time when the state was far more generous in its support of higher education.

During the years that Jordan attended CSU, higher education accounted for more than 20 percent of the state's general fund budget. That dropped to just over 10 percent in the years leading up to the Great Recession in 2008. Since then it has dropped to only 6.4 percent of the state's general fund budget, though funding from ARRA has helped offset some of the funding lost during the past two years.[55] Absent a new stimulus plan, however, that federal assistance will soon disappear.

Recognizing all the benefits and good fortune that both Jordan and New Belgium Brewing have received over the years, Jordan takes to heart a quote from Luke 12:48, "For everyone to whom much is given, of him shall much be required." And giving back is a fundamental aspect of how New Belgium operates:

> It's about making sure that we pay a living wage, sharing profits with our co-workers, sharing equity through ESOP (Employee Stock Ownership Plan) ownership, giving people a bike, providing domestic partner benefits, having paternity and maternity leave, having a generous personal time-off plan—I could go on. . . . [This set of company policies] comes from the belief: (1) that to whom much is given, much is required, (2) that excessive consumption is really not the best mark of a life well-lived, (3) that the pooling of labor to build equity should inure at least at some level to the benefit of everyone, and (4) that the accounting for our impact on the commons is our responsibility to work toward. . . . I'd never want to sit here and say, "Oh yeah, we account for all of our impact"—because we don't. But we understand it to be a process, and we are into continuous improvement, so in that area as well as many others we continue to invest money and intellectual energy and passion and focus.

We lift up a pint in celebration of Jordan's uncompromising values and business success.

Anirvan Chatterjee: Leaving the Ladder Down behind Him

Anirvan Chatterjee is the founder and the CEO of BookFinder.com,
which later became a subsidiary of Amazon.com.[56]

Anirvan Chatterjee didn't set out to found a successful online business as a young technologist in Silicon Valley in the 1990s, but it
almost seemed inevitable:

> I'd been running the site as a hobby project out of my dorm
> room, and it started growing, gaining users. Meanwhile it felt
> like everyone around me was trying to start their own dot-coms.
> I don't have an entrepreneurial background in my family. But
> the entrepreneurial dream was totally a part of San Francisco
> Bay Area culture during those early dot-com years, with every-
> one reading their *Wired* magazines and talking about how the
> Internet would change the world. It was hard not to get caught up.

The result was BookFinder.com, a comparison search engine
for new, used, rare, and out-of-print books that the then-19-year-
old Chatterjee first built as a class project at UC Berkeley and
which eventually became a subsidiary of Amazon.com.

A similar environmental boost came from his family: his
father, who had emigrated from India to Canada and then moved
to the Bay Area, was an engineer.

> I started programming when I was 15. My dad worked tech jobs,
> and he was able to bring a computer home from his work on
> the weekends, until we bought our first computer. My parents
> had moved so that I could go to school in a well-funded public
> school district. Property prices were higher, but they made that
> sacrifice for my education. I started taking computer science
> classes at school as early as possible. We had a great computer
> science teacher, and she really sparked my interest in trying to
> think about how people use technology.

In fact, state-sponsored education played a multigenerational
role in Chatterjee's success. The Indian government trained his
father (and thousands of others) in engineering, ultimately helping

fuel technological advances in the United States and elsewhere. Once the Chatterjees came to America, California's public schools nourished and focused Anirvan's nascent interest in computers.

When Chatterjee was trying to decide whether to take his entrepreneurial leap from college to business, he sought and received the encouragement and the blessings of his mentors at UC Berkeley, the flagship university of California's public higher-education system. "The support of my professors meant a lot to me," he says. "Many of them had seen me start the project as an undergrad and continue working on it as a grad student, seeing the site grow, seeing it get national attention. It meant so much to get that kind of support from them, letting me use the site as an example project in my classes."

Before the Internet, finding rare books was a hit-or-miss affair of hours spent searching the dusty stacks of mom-and-pop stores. The digital revolution allowed individual retailers to widely share their catalogs, but comparison-shopping was still difficult. That was the problem BookFinder.com was created to solve. "There were over 50 different sites where individual bookstores could upload their catalogs," says Chatterjee. "What BookFinder.com offered was a one-stop search. As a user you would type in the name of the book you wanted, and we'd instantly search millions of books for sale and show you all the choices, so you could pick the cheapest copy or a signed first edition or whatever you wanted. You could then buy the book of your choice directly from the bookseller."

Public investment in libraries served as a source of inspiration:

> If it weren't for libraries, I may not have been reading so heavily or have gotten into the bookselling business. Growing up, my parents would take me to the library every week, and I got so much joy in being able to check out any book I wanted. I'm a voracious reader. I read over a hundred books a year. The mix has changed over time. After I started working, I started buying more of those books, and now the mix is about 50-50. But libraries sustained me to the point where I started taking buying books seriously enough that I could start a business around it.

Chatterjee stayed with his company after it was bought out—first by used-book search giant Abebooks and then ultimately by Amazon.com—but he left in 2009, after almost 13 years at the helm, to spend the next year doing citizen journalism with his wife, focusing on global climate change issues.

Chatterjee attributes his success to factors beyond talent and hard work: "Being there at the right time, at the right place, with the right idea had a lot to do with it. I mean, I worked hard. I don't want to discount the fact that I worked incredibly hard on my startup. But a lot of people work incredibly hard on their ideas, and people work hard all their lives and don't necessarily have much to show for it financially at the end of their lives. So I count myself as incredibly lucky."

Ironically for an American story, even Chatterjee's brown skin helped him: in the world of Internet startups, his Indian-American ancestry gave him the reassuringly "right look" for a computer programmer in Silicon Valley. "My race and gender certainly didn't hurt," he says.

He also cites hard-to-measure yet still very real "public goods"—such as the enforceability of contracts—as part of the environment that allowed his business to thrive:

> As a really young company, we'd end up juggling 50 to 100 contracts at any given time with companies in the book space. In many cases, we would contract with a company so that they would have their books listed on our site at no cost, and they would pay us something if and only if we helped them sell any books. But we couldn't really know if we'd helped sell any books or not. Once our users left our website, we had no way of knowing if they completed the transaction. But we trusted those contracts. It meant a lot to be working in a stable business environment in a first-world country, where we felt like we could rely on partners to honor contracts.

Similarly, just as his company relied on the established legal framework and the centuries of contract law and practice to

It meant a lot to be working in a stable business environment in a first-world country, where we felt like we could rely on partners to honor contracts.

— ANIRVAN CHATTERJEE

undergird its business relationships as a programmer. Chatterjee is well aware that he was able to draw from the commons to design and engineer his website. "We didn't have to write 99 percent of the code for the BookFinder.com platform," he says. "We built on top of an open source operating system, databases, programming language, and code libraries. Thousands of programmers had banded together to build great software and give it away at no cost. That meant we didn't have to spend $50,000 buying a license from Oracle—we could download a free database and get started building a company, thanks to a generous sharing economy."

Just as he acknowledges the role of good luck in his success, Chatterjee recognizes the bad luck that can trip up others.

A supporter therefore of public services that give a necessary hand up, he bemoans the recent "massive disinvestment" in the California public education system that served him so well:

> That [disinvestment in public education] starts at K–12 and goes all the way up to our two tiers of public universities and community colleges. And having started a business that came out of a university class project, it seems only fair that others have that same opportunity to access a space that could be an incubator for every Californian with a great idea. I didn't think I'd start a business—I just happened upon it. I was at the right time and place but in an environment where I was inspired to go further. And I really hope that's going to be as accessible as possible to a large, diverse audience.

He says that California's public universities are addressing funding shortages by filling classrooms with more full-tuition, out-of-state students, leaving fewer slots for local students whose education is partially subsidized by the state: "Our taxpayer dollars should be supporting more in-state students getting this kind of public education. It's not only for those who can pay more. . . . Yeah, I've gotten a lot and I want to make sure others have that as well."

On a national scale too, Chatterjee thinks it's simple logic that public services be paid for by those best able to bear the cost—people like him, who often have been the beneficiaries of those services:

> I've been incredibly lucky, building and selling a small dot-com in my twenties. Especially in a recession like this, people like me are the first ones who should be tapped to make sure that the country's able to pay for its basic human needs. . . . So, yeah, I am very much in favor of substantially increased progressive taxation, possibly a tax on wealth or a tax on financial transactions. There's a huge class of Americans who can afford to be tapped a little bit more so we can pull everyone else up with us.

Chatterjee believes in leaving the ladder down behind him.

Building the Internet

The success of many of the individuals and businesses featured in this book is intimately tied to the emergence and the widespread use of the Internet. Bill Gates's Microsoft Corporation would be on a dramatically different trajectory were it not for the Internet. Anirvan Chatterjee's BookFinder.com, which he later sold to Amazon.com, would not exist without the Internet. Hanna Andersson, the children's clothing company founded by Gun Denhart (profiled later in this book), makes more than 90 percent of its nonstore sales over the Internet.

But the Internet did not just appear by some magic or the "invisible hand" of market forces. The Internet is unquestionably a creation of governmental action. The Internet traces its history back to the 1960s and the work of the Defense Advanced Research Projects Agency of the Department of Defense, later renamed simply the Advanced Research Projects Agency (ARPA) as "a future-oriented funder of 'high-risk, high-gain' research."[57]

With the funding of ARPA, computers at four major universities in the Southwest were connected in 1969 to form ARPANET. This was expanded shortly thereafter to include other universities and research institutes. Through ARPA and other public institutions, our tax dollars would fund vital research that led to the creation of new technologies and protocols like TCP/IP, ASCII, FTP, routers, and the now ubiquitous e-mail convention *username@host.domain* that laid the foundation of the Internet, a term coined for the first time in 1974.[58]

The vital public role in creating the Internet did not end with these early innovations. The National Science Foundation (NSF)—a federal agency created by Congress in 1950 "to promote the progress of science; to advance the national health, prosperity, and welfare; to secure the national defense"[59]—would play a key role as well. In the 1980s and 1990s, the NSF helped broadly expand the Internet, first through the creation of CSNet in 1981, which connected many more universities to ARPANET, and later with the creation of NSFNet in 1986 as "a cross-country 56 Kbps backbone for the Internet. They maintained their sponsorship [of NSFNet] for nearly a decade, setting rules for its non-commercial government and research uses."[60]

By 1995 the Internet had made the switch to commercial, for-profit business, with most traffic now going through servers owned by AOL, CompuServe, and other companies instead of the NSF backbone. The NSF remained involved, however, in expanding access to the Internet in K–12 schools and local public libraries as well as conducting research on "high volume connections."[61]

Today innovation and expansion of the Internet continue to be driven in part through public action and taxpayer support. Among the notable challenges facing the Internet today are the broad swaths of the United States where access to high-speed Internet is limited or nonexistent, including nearly one-third of rural America[62] and many low-income urban communities. Current efforts to expand access to high-speed Internet are being driven by the Rural Utilities Service of the US Department of Agriculture (USDA) through an ongoing loan and grant program and through regulatory reforms of the FCC.[63]

While many private companies and researchers were involved along the way, the story of the Internet is fundamentally a story of publicly funded research and development.

Peter Barnes: Wealth Comes out of the Commons

Peter Barnes co-founded Working Assets and is currently
a writer and an entrepreneur in Point Reyes, California.[64]

Peter Barnes co-founded Working Assets, a financial services and telephone company serving progressive investors and consumers. Like his parents, Barnes attended New York City public schools, and "the fact that my father, a penniless son of immigrants, could get a really good free education certainly benefited me." After graduating from Harvard in 1962, Barnes worked as a journalist for 15 years and then decided to become a businessman. In 1982 he co-founded Working Assets as a socially responsible investment firm that later moved into credit cards and telephone service. He sold his stock in Working Assets to his partners and retired in 1995. His experience as a business owner led him to co-found OnTheCommons.org, an organization dedicated to expanding popular understanding of the "commons," which includes, in Barnes's words, "the gifts of nature and society that we share and inherit together—and have an obligation to pass on to our heirs, undiminished and more or less equally." This notion of the commons includes environmental assets such as the air, fisheries, water, and land. It also includes socially created assets such as our highways, legal system, the Internet, and accumulated scientific knowledge.[65]

Barnes's understanding of the role of the commons has shaped his perspective about wealth creation. The notion that stock values are in part socially rather than individually created will be new to most readers. It comes from his experience taking (or rather *almost* taking) Working Assets public:

> What we, the private shareholders, learned was that our business was worth a whole lot more as a public company than as a private company. What added this extra value? It wasn't that we'd make more sales or profit—these numbers would be the same either way. The extra value came purely from the fact that our stock would be *liquid*—we could sell it to any Tom, Dick, or Harriet, any day of the week. According to our investment banker, liquidity alone would add 30 percent to the value of our stock.[66]

Though in the end they decided not to take the company public, for Barnes it was a pivotal lesson. "That added value comes not from the company itself but from society—from the stock market and the infrastructure of government, financial institutions, and media that supports it." For many whose wealth has been created in the stock market, it is easy to forget that this entire system has been built over several generations and is regulated at taxpayer expense through institutions such as the Securities and Exchange Commission.

And the US stock market is not just local. It is a highly sophisticated global marketplace where you can sell your shares virtually anywhere at any time. This gives access to an infinitely larger market of potential buyers—the market for shares becomes the whole world. This greatly increases liquidity and value. As Barnes points out, "You are plugged into a global network; you get listed, and based on your filings with the Securities and Exchange Commission, people generally believe your numbers. You talk to a few analysts and, sight unseen, they pay you money. It's a wonderful social creation that basically rewards private shareholders for adding their company to the grand casino that is the publicly traded stock market."

For Barnes the stock market is just one of the ways in which a private enterprise benefits from society's investment and infrastructure. The entire system of institutions that fosters trust in the marketplace is essential. When Barnes co-founded Working Assets as a money market fund, he created advertisements to attract investors: "The next thing we knew, people were sending us big checks in plain envelopes. These people had never seen me before, nor met anyone from our company. They didn't know us from a hole in the wall. So they didn't trust *us*. They trusted a *system* that took centuries to build. I wrote some ads, but no one would have responded to them without the whole infrastructure that gave people trust."

Repeated examples show what happens when this trust in the marketplace is shaken. In the wake of the Enron and WorldCom scandals, millions of investors lost confidence in the accuracy of corporate accounting, and the stock market lost 28 percent of its value.[67] A study by the Brookings Institution estimated that the decline in investor confidence cost the economy approximately $35 billion.[68] "The corporate scandals caused people to stop trusting the numbers that companies were reporting," said Barnes.

PHOTO COURTESY OF PETER BARNES

People were sending us big checks in plain envelopes. . . . They didn't know us from a hole in the wall. So they didn't trust us. They trusted a system *that took centuries to build.*

— PETER BARNES

"Imagine how much value is created by trust and the whole system that assures that trust?"

Since leaving Working Assets, Barnes has focused his energies on writing about economics and the commons. He is the author of *Who Owns the Sky?*, a book proposing a solution for environmental degradation and economic inequality called the "sky trust." Recognizing the air as a common asset that absorbs pollution, Barnes calls for using the proceeds from selling pollution rights to fund wealth-building accounts for everyone. He helped write "cap and dividend" legislation that would charge polluters and return the revenue to everyone on a one-person, one-share basis. Barnes believes this would curb global warming and ensure a strong middle class at the same time.

Barnes is an advocate of a healthy capitalism that recognizes the value of the commons. This value is huge and lies behind much of what we call "private" wealth. "Most wealth comes out of the commons," he says, "and individuals add a little bit on top of that. But because of the way capitalism is set up, for adding that little bit, you get to grab an enormous share of what comes out of the commons."

This description by Barnes reflects what we mean when we talk of the built-together reality of individual and business success. In our case, we're speaking primarily of the public infrastructure, built through generations of public investments in the common good. Whatever the entrepreneur adds is built on top of that foundation.

For Barnes the challenge of capitalism in the twenty-first century is to recognize the value that is created by the commons and to protect it—give it standing and clout. There will still be those who generate substantial individual wealth, but it won't be because they have pocketed the wealth of the commons.[69]

Amy Domini: Regulation Makes My Industry Possible

Amy Domini is founder and president of the Domini Social Equity Fund, creator of the Domini 400 Social Index, and founder of the Domini Social Investment mutual fund.[70]

Amy Domini questions a lot of things. She challenges the status quo on a regular basis; in fact, questioning the status quo forms the basis of her groundbreaking business. But ask her to point to the influences that made her an entrepreneur, an advocate, a pioneer, and a challenger, and she'll tell you it was the public structures and the predictable social order of small-town 1950s childhood in suburban Connecticut that instilled in her a sense of safety, clarity, duty, and service. "Everybody went to Girl Scouts," she says. "Everybody went to church and Sunday School. Everybody learned how to figure-skate; everybody learned how to swim. . . . If you didn't want to go stir-crazy, you were always interacting with other people. . . . In my mother's generation [it was] creating a bridge club or a PTA [Parent/Teacher Association]."

One of Domini's lessons about the role of public investment came early. She was the daughter of a public school teacher and the owner of an eggplant processing plant. Domini recalls, as a teenager, her parents pressing their fellow taxpayers to approve a tax levy to build a new high school. The levy failed and the new school was not built, leaving the students to suffer in a dilapidated building. "It was one of the first times I made the connection between paying taxes and the quality of life."

Her path to becoming a broker in a male-dominated industry was not without help but also not without hard work. With the help of her grandfather, she got a job as a clerk, making copies at a brokerage firm. Using the lessons from her childhood, she arrived five minutes early to work and meetings, did a little bit more than asked, and eventually got promoted through the secretarial ranks. In 1974 she recalls that the stock market was "in the tank"; and although most brokers at the time were men, she asked her boss if she could take the training and to her surprise soon became the firm's first female broker. She later learned that four women had sued Merrill Lynch for gender discrimination and realized she was probably an indirect beneficiary of those women's exercising their rights.

In those days, she says, stock ideas would often come "over a squawk box from some smart person in New York" and then be passed on to clients to see if they wanted to invest. Domini found that some of her clients were offended to be offered stock in weapons manufacturers or tobacco, activities that conflicted with their own values: "You are always supposed to know your customers, where they live, et cetera. I just added to it: 'Is there something you don't want me to talk about, or something you have deep commitments to, or something you don't want to be an investor in?' Virtually everyone said yes. I was amazed."

This simple but powerful twist on the staid and conservative investment field became her niche and ultimately blossomed into the growing socially responsible investment field of today.

As a young stockbroker, Domini built her client base in part by teaching adult education classes in the evening. She drew up a course called "Ethical Investing," which she offered alongside the "ABCs of Investing" class she was teaching. Soon after, she co-authored the groundbreaking 1984 book by the same title (after overcoming her disbelief that no such book already existed!). In subsequent years she would continue this groundbreaking work, as described by Domini Social Investments:

> Amy realized that what social investors needed was a bench-mark—something akin to traditional investment benchmarks like the Standard & Poor's 500 or the Dow Jones Industrial Average—that could be used to determine whether there was a cost or a benefit, in dollars and cents, to invest this way. For example, would an investor who chose not to invest in tobacco companies or major polluters, preferring companies with bet-ter environmental and human rights records, perform better or worse than investors who did not consider these factors? She saw this uncertainty as the primary obstacle to the growth of socially responsible investing.
>
> In 1989, she and her partners Peter Kinder and Steve Lydenberg began work on the Domini 400 Social Index, an index of 400 primarily large-cap US corporations, roughly comparable to the S&P 500, selected based on a wide range of social and envi-ronmental standards. When it was launched in 1990, it was the first index of its kind. A year later, they launched the Domini Social Equity Fund to provide investors with a fund that tracks the Index.[71]

Although it comes as no surprise to Domini, these socially responsible investments performed as well as or better than tradi-tional investment portfolios.[72]

Far from bristling at the regulation of her industry, Domini speaks with a seeming sense of pride at the extent to which the mutual fund industry is regulated by the Securities and Exchange Commission. The whole mutual fund industry and its investors

PHOTO BY PAK WONG

The mutual fund industry is a regulated industry. People who complain about regulation don't even know what regulation is; it's consumer protection.

— AMY DOMINI

benefit from this extensive regulation, even if many of us take it for granted:

> The industry I am in, the mutual fund industry, is a regulated industry. People who complain about regulation don't even know what regulation is; it's consumer protection. That's its purpose. I must do reporting to my board and shareholders on a quarterly basis. My calendar is full of follow-through on mandatory reporting. Still, if you were to say to me, "Which of these regulations would you strip away?" I'd tell you that I am fine with them.
>
> If I were an investor and had an inkling of an understanding of how regulated a mutual fund is compared with other financial management routes, I would be stunned. A financial planner is somewhat regulated; a hedge fund almost totally unregulated—nothing to keep them from being liars, cheaters, thieves, except perhaps laws against fraud or insider trading. The regulatory

environment is great consumer protection. In this tough market, where consumers don't feel protected, [regulation of mutual funds] should give them some comfort.

Domini's companies, and the whole socially responsible investing field, also benefit *indirectly* from government-mandated disclosures and regulation of other industries.

I could not have started my business without federally mandated disclosures. For instance, if I am trying to evaluate a company, I look to the company's own reporting. There is a lot of it. I particularly look at the Form 10K. Corporations must by SEC guidelines release quarterly information, reports, and the annual reports must be audited. The 10K [report required by all publicly traded companies] tells me a lot. But many other sources grow from mandatory reporting.

How many people died in the workplace last year? That is federally mandated disclosure, so that it is available to me in most cases. Are there any environmental liabilities? I look to the 10K, which must by law reveal this (though it is admittedly under-reported). Further, the Toxic Release Inventory [is a] federally mandated data source.

Who are the top officers by pay? In today's cyber-age it takes about a nanosecond to find out if there are any women or people of color in that top five by pay, and their names are disclosed due to regulation. The board, ditto—federal mandate.

What product safety recalls have occurred? Regulations mean that the information is disclosed, but it is not easy to find. Thankfully, Public Justice, the group that lobbies on behalf of consumers, has a list on their website, which makes it easy. Does the company sell weapons? Weapons procurement is federally disclosed.

Not only do my investors know that the product I offer has robust federal oversight, but I know that the data I rely upon to create that product does as well.

Free-market theory assumes falsely that people have *perfect information* about the products they are buying, which is necessary for people to make rational choices between competing products. In the real world though, perfect information is almost never available to consumers. Most consumers have little idea about where the products they buy come from or how they were made. The same applies to investors.

The regulatory examples Domini lifts up help make up for that flaw in market theory by gathering valuable information, which Domini uses as the cornerstone of her business model. This is much the same concept used by the USDA in requiring companies to label food products with a list of ingredients and nutritional information. For markets to even come close to functioning as theorized, this kind of transparency is necessary, but it rarely comes without government involvement.

REALITY CHECK

Government Regulation in Finance

For businesses to launch, expand, and thrive, they need access to capital. In the short term, bank loans are often used to fund the purchase of a new building, new manufacturing equipment, or inventory. Over the long term, businesses can go to the stock market, selling shares of their company on the market through an IPO to generate capital for large-scale expansion efforts. Both the banking industry and the stock market rely on the regulatory environment provided through governmental action to provide stability and consumer confidence to the system. When financial markets fail, the consequences are severe.

The stock market crash of 1929 brought the entire economy to a standstill. At the time, there was nothing to prohibit banks from investing depositor money in the market. Immediately after the crash, people rushed to withdraw what was left of their money, and consequently many banks became insolvent; 40 percent of banks failed.[73] This was the onset of the Great Depression, which had global impacts.

Congress responded with a wave of new regulations designed to bring stability to the financial system. In 1933 Congress created the Securities and Exchange Commission to create and enforce rules that promote financial transparency and give investors access to knowledge pertinent to investing.[74] On the banking front, Congress passed the Glass-Steagall Act, which among other things prohibited commercial banks from engaging in risky investment activities, and created the Federal Deposit Insurance Corporation (FDIC) to guarantee customer deposits.[75] These regulations helped restore confidence in a financial system that had been discredited by the stock market crash of 1929.

Bank runs, financial crises, and ensuing periods of recession and depression became briefer and less frequent in the prosperous decades after the Great Depression.[76] A wave of anti-government sentiment that started in the 1970s culminated in 1999 with the deregulation of the financial sector through the passage of the Gramm-Leach-Bliley Act, which effectively repealed the core provisions of Glass-Steagall.[77] The legal barrier between investment and commercial banking was broken down, allowing for an explosion of profits and risk in the financial industry. As substantial as the monetary gains were, the opportunity for loss was just as significant. Banks and investors made money after 1999, but, interestingly, the market has crashed twice since then (2000 and 2008).

After the market crash in 2008, banks again seized up. Congress addressed the immediate credit crisis through the Troubled Asset Relief Program (TARP); it then began the process of reregulating the financial markets to ensure greater transparency and stability by passing the Dodd-Frank Act in 2010.[78] The sweeping financial reform law established a Consumer Financial Protection Bureau, among other things, but it did not restore the key provisions of Glass-Steagall to curtail excessive risk in the banking sector.

Regulation of banks and the economy has been paramount to the success of the individuals profiled in this book. Without functioning banks, businesses cannot get loans. Without transparency of financial markets, confidence is lost. Warren Buffett's wealth came from his work in tightly regulated stock and equity markets. Jerry Fiddler and Amy Domini both credit the regulation of finance and the SEC with a role in their success. Jim Sherblom (profiled later in this book), former CFO of Genzyme, points out that SEC regulation encourages competition by ensuring that the game investors play is "a fair and open game, and everybody can have confidence in the system."[79]

Virtually all of the entrepreneurs profiled in this book have benefited from the government regulation of finance, as well as the creation of the SEC, in ways that are often taken for granted. The US economy simply cannot function properly or efficiently without the stability, transparency, and confidence that strong and effective regulation of the financial industry provides.

Nikhil Arora: It Takes a Village to Raise a Business

Nikhil Arora is the co-founder and the co-owner of Back to the Roots, an Oakland-based sustainable-products company.[80]

Nikhil Arora was born in 1986, making him the youngest entrepreneur profiled in this book. He is the co-founder, along with Alejandro Velez, of Back to the Roots, a startup business in Oakland, California, that was "inspired by the idea of turning waste into wages and fresh, local food."[81] In 2010 they were one of Social Venture Network's Innovation Award winners,[82] and in 2011 Arora and Velez were named among CNN Money's "10 Generation Next Entrepreneurs to Watch"[83]—and for good reason. Only two years old, their hallmark product—kits to grow gourmet mushrooms entirely from used coffee grounds—is already being sold in nearly 500 stores nationwide, including 300 Whole Foods stores, 150 independents, and, most recently, in 30 Home Depot stores for test marketing in Northern California.

Arora is a first-generation Indian American who was born and raised in Southern California. His parents both graduated from college in India, and his father received a master's degree at a university in Germany. Both landed professional, computer-related jobs after moving to the United States, providing Arora with a solid middle-class upbringing. Arora, like many business leaders featured in this book, attended public schools, both in Southern California and when he went on to study political science and business at UC Berkeley.

It was there, in his final semester at UC Berkeley, that he met his business partner, Alejandro Velez. They both heard their professor make a comment in a business ethics class about its being possible to grow gourmet mushrooms entirely from used coffee grounds. Independently, they both approached their professor, asking if he had any more information. The professor responded to each of them separately via e-mail: "I have no idea, but this other kid asked me that, too. You guys should link up." They did.[84]

Shortly after they met, they began experimenting and grew their first batch of oyster mushrooms. Eventually, the business plan began to take shape, with used coffee grounds supplied by Peet's Coffee & Tea, good-quality gourmet mushrooms grown by the company, and customers to buy them, including Whole Foods. But with less than $2,000 of their own money to start with, an initial grant they received from UC Berkeley made a big difference. "I think we were fortunate enough at that point—a couple of weeks before graduation," says Arora. "We got a small grant of $5,000 from our chancellor for social innovation. We looked at each other and said, 'You know what? We have *got* to do this!' And that's really how we became full-time mushroom farmers."[85]

The grant from UC Berkeley's Haas School of Business was not the last grant they would receive. In subsequent years they won other grants of between $10,000 and $50,000 as a result of contests to identify new ideas, as well as competitive awards targeting young and urban entrepreneurs. The funding for these grants was largely made possible through public-private partnerships, a recurring theme Arora brought up in our interview with him.

Shortly after the initial success in growing and selling gourmet mushrooms, Back to the Roots moved into producing mushroom-growing kits. Through the kits—boxes of preseeded coffee grounds

PHOTO BY KRISTEN LOKEN PHOTOGRAPHY

We got a small grant of $5,000 from our chancellor for social innovation. We looked at each other and said, "You know what? We have got to do this!" And that's really how we became full-time mushroom farmers.

— NIKHIL ARORA
(right, with business partner Alejandro Velez)

that customers simply moisten to start growing—they dramatically expanded the reach of their business, which now includes a 10,000 square foot warehouse in addition to their nationally distributed product.

Arora also speaks of the importance of the loans they were able to get in the critical first years of their business. In addition to a $25,000 loan from Whole Foods to promote local producers, they received a $50,000 loan through the Oakland Business Development Center (OBDC). The OBDC loan program uses public funds from the City of Oakland, the federal SBA microloan program, and others. The purpose of the OBDC loan program is captured on its website: "We finance businesses that help to achieve positive social, environmental, and financial impact in the communities we serve. Our mission-driven loans increase job

opportunities in low-to-moderate-income areas, foster entrepreneurship among underserved groups, and bolster economic and
community development through the transformation of blighted
neighborhoods."[86]

Arora points to the JOBS NOW! program as an example of a
public-private partnership that helped his new business grow
while providing the long-term unemployed with a chance to get
back into the workforce. The JOBS NOW! program, administered
by the San Francisco Human Services Agency, initially received
80 percent of its funds through the American Recovery and
Reinvestment Act, also known as the federal stimulus bill.[87]

The jobs program paid the salaries, for an initial period of
time, of new, prequalified employees who had been out of work
for six months or longer and had children under 18 years of age.
Federal funding for the program expired in 2010 and was not
renewed, but the City of San Francisco found new funding for the
program at the state and local levels. Under the renewed program,
an employer can be reimbursed for the first $5,000 in salary for
individuals hired through the jobs program.

Arora notes that Back to the Roots participated in both the initial federally funded program as well as the locally funded, scaled-
back version of the program. More than 60 percent of the people
they hired through the program became long-term employees.
Speaking of the program's benefits, Arora states, "We were able to
get subsidized for that $5,000, which is nice because it pays for all
that training period, which is the most inefficient part of bringing
someone on. It really incentivized us to hire, to grow, and to take
some chances because we had the people who could help us do it.
I can't tell you how instrumental that program was for us, more
than any other grants we received. It was the most tangible form of
support: helping pay the people you're hiring."

A brief glance at Arora's story shows the ways in which public and private factors have contributed to his business success. In
addition to his and Velez's hard work and entrepreneurial spirit,

Arora has benefited from a host of public institutions, including the public school system, UC Berkeley, public-private grants
for innovation, the OBDC loan program, and the San Francisco
JOBS NOW! program.

Reflecting on the success of Back to the Roots, Arora reiterates
the value of the public-private partnerships, direct public supports,
and all the other businesses—from Whole Foods to Peet's Coffee
& Tea—nonprofits, and individuals that have supported them on
their journey: "You know that saying about how it takes a village to
raise a child? Well, I think it takes a village to raise a business too."

Ben Cohen: Holding the Business in Trust for the Community

*Ben Cohen is a co-founder of Ben & Jerry's ice cream
company, based in Waterbury, Vermont.*[88]

Ben Cohen's rapid-fire recitation of his résumé can only bring a
smile and a sense of amazement. Perhaps it's where he learned to
value the work of the common man:

> I went to public school in Merrick, on Long Island, and after
> that I went to Colgate University for a year and a half, dropped
> out, went to a few other places and dropped out of all of them,
> and, you know, had a bunch of jobs along the way. I was a news
> paper boy. I worked at McDonald's. I worked sorting mail, as a
> Pinkerton Guard, an assistant superintendent, a garbage man,
> a Yellow Pages deliveryman, and a night mopper at a Jamesway
> department store. I was a short-order cook, a taxicab driver in
> New York, and a clerk at a hospital. I was a pottery wheel deliv-
> erer, and I tried to make a living selling pottery, but nobody
> would buy my pottery. My first real job was at a residential
> school for emotionally disturbed kids in Upstate New York as
> a crafts teacher.

Cohen never expected to make it big in the world of ice
cream. In fact, when he teamed up with his childhood buddy Jerry

Greenfield ("We met in seventh-grade gym class, running around the track; we were the two slowest, fattest kids in the class"), ice cream was supposed to be just a stepping-stone to something more desirable: "We decided to try out being in business for ourselves and opened a homemade-ice-cream parlor. The idea was that it was just going to be a little one-storefront operation, and then we'd sell it in a couple years, and with the money we got, we'd buy a tractor-trailer and become cross-country truck drivers."

They started the business on just $12,000: $2,000 borrowed from Cohen's father, $2,000 of his own, $4,000 from Greenfield, and a $4,000 bank loan. Drawing on Greenfield's biochemistry background and a college textbook simply called *Ice Cream,* they began cranking out "gobs of homemade ice cream," searching for the right formula.

Neither Cohen nor Greenfield had much background in commerce. They consulted with the University of Vermont, and Cohen took a $5 correspondence course from Penn State University.

> The way we got our business stuff was by mail from the Small Business Administration. The SBA published all these little pamphlets. They cost 25 cents apiece, and they were on all the different aspects of a small business. Whatever you needed to know, it was there, in one of these little pamphlets. And you know, there was no bullshit in 'em. They were excellent.
>
> Jerry and I devoured the SBA pamphlets that the government puts out on how to start a business and how to conduct business. It just educated us about every phase of business, from selecting a location to marketing and advertising and bookkeeping and creating a business plan. So that was quite helpful to us.
>
> And then, at a stage when Ben & Jerry's needed money, we ended up getting an Urban Development Action Grant from the government.

Being in the food business brings its own set of concerns, and Cohen recognizes the importance of government's role here as

Who created the wealth? It was really created by our customers and employees, people who worked with us.

— BEN COHEN

well: "The government does set food-safety regulations, and we found those to be helpful. It taught us how to make safe products, and it certainly was helpful in making sure all the suppliers and vendors had to make safe products that conformed to the government's standards."

Reflecting on the role of government in supporting a business like theirs, he adds: "Every business needs the infrastructure that government provides in terms of roads and transportation. And I think [another role is] just refereeing a level playing field and setting down the rules by which businesses can go about their business."

Cohen and Greenfield could be forgiven if they believed that their success *was* purely the result of their individual effort. The first years of the business were quite a struggle, and winters in Burlington, Vermont, were particularly bad for selling ice cream.

So they began selling 2.5-gallon tubs to restaurants out of the back of Cohen's car. They eventually hit upon packaging their product in the printed pint containers for which they are now famous and selling it to mom-and-pop stores. They went from 50 accounts to 200 accounts in a matter of months, and took off from there.

Soon the business was bursting at the seams, with not enough room to store raw ingredients or finished product, not to mention "lousy" working conditions. Rather than go the standard route and take in venture capital, they decided to get money from the community. They held the first-ever in-state Vermont IPO "against the advice of the lawyers, accountants, and business advisers":

> There came a time in the history of Ben & Jerry's when we needed a cash infusion to grow the business. And the normal route for doing that would have been to take in an investment from a venture capitalist, but Jerry and I didn't want to do that because instead of making a few already-wealthy people wealthier, we wanted to find a way for the community to become the owners of the business; we wanted to spread the wealth and share the wealth.

> The idea was to find a way for our neighbors—essentially Vermonters, people who had supported us from the very beginning—to become the owners of Ben & Jerry's. And the way we found to do that was to hold what became the first-ever in-state Vermont public stock offering, so we sold shares to Vermonters for a very low minimum buy. I think the minimum buy was $126 to get in on the ground floor of this IPO, which was usually an opportunity reserved for wealthier, sophisticated investors.

> We advertised and sold these shares direct to everyday Vermonters, advertising them in the first section of the newspaper along with the clothing ads and the supermarket ads. And by the end of the offering, one out of every 100 Vermont families had become an owner of Ben & Jerry's.

That money built the first plant in Waterbury. From that point on, Cohen believed he was "holding the business in trust for the community." The uniqueness of Cohen and Greenfield's relationship to their investors was reflected in their annual meetings, which had the flavor of celebrations and attracted thousands of shareholders. Says Cohen, "Most companies hold their meetings in out-of-the-way places at out-of-the-way times and try not to have anybody show up. We did everything we could to get as many people to come as possible."

Employees too received different treatment at Ben & Jerry's. Despite working 16-hour days, the two founders had modest salaries and did not receive dividends or profits while they were running the company. They also had a compressed salary ratio that started at 5-to-1, then moved to 7-to-1, meaning that the CEO could only be paid a maximum of seven times what the lowest-paid worker was making. "We had a profit-sharing system because we believed that the employees should share in the profits because *they* were creating the profits. And we had a foundation that was run by the employees. They decided where the money should be given."

It's not that Cohen takes none of the credit for the success of the enterprise, it's just that he keeps it in perspective. When pressed to identify his personal skills and talents, he responds, "Drive, perseverance, focus, passionate dedication, self-sacrifice, somewhat of a talent for marketing, a passionate desire to integrate social concerns into our day-to-day business activities, and an intuitive sense of what kind of ice cream people would like to eat!"

But he recognizes the relative value of all types of work and doesn't believe that the rewards of one should be astronomically different from those of another:

> Yeah, we put our life into it. Yeah, I was working 16 hours a day; but the people who were working for me, they were working eight hours a day. Yeah, I was working *twice* as much. But the people working for me were working *hard*. When I put in a day of mental work, I'm not working any harder than somebody on my production floor who's putting in eight hours a day of

physical work in an environment that's a helluva lot worse than my office.

Who created the wealth? It was really created by our customers and employees, people who worked with us. And when the company went public, we did grant a bunch of stock to the people who were working at the company at the time.

Ben & Jerry's was sold in 1999 to the multinational Unilever for about $326 million.[89] Cohen was opposed to the sale and believes that the more recently enacted B Corporation law in Vermont might have allowed them to remain independent.[90] But some parts of the social mission were continued, and he was happy to see the company recently announce that it would source most of its nondairy ingredients through fair-trade methods, which will affect farmers all around the world. Cohen's share of the proceeds was about $40 million. How does he view that money? "I always worked on the idea that 50 percent of the money that I get goes back to the community in the form of advocating for progressive social change—to change the system so that we don't end up with as many people in poverty and needing remedial welfare-type bailouts. I believe very strongly, and I've got this quote up on my wall: 'If we had justice, we wouldn't need charity.' So I use 50 percent of the money I get to try to achieve that."

Gun Denhart: Healthy Communities Support Healthy Businesses

Gun Denhart founded the Hanna Andersson
clothing company in Portland, Oregon.[91]

Gun Denhart grew up in a small university town in southern Sweden. She learned from watching her father, a businessman who eventually started his own company in the packaging business. At university, she planned on studying law but quickly discovered she was better at business: "It was kind of in my genes."

After meeting her husband, Tom, a native of Portland, Oregon, the two settled in Greenwich, Connecticut, where they had their first child in 1980. Denhart recalls, "We dressed him in Swedish clothes, and people kept stopping me in the street to ask, 'Where did you get those clothes?'" Neither Gun nor Tom had experience with clothing or mail-order businesses, but they moved to Portland in 1983 and launched Hanna Andersson as a tiny mail-order catalog offering high-quality children's clothing.

"We didn't know anything about children's clothes or about mail order," says Denhart. "But we were lucky because that was just when the Baby Boomers were having a lot of children. There were a lot of synthetics in children's clothing, and we were different because we used all-natural fibers. People liked what we had because the quality was really great and we offered bright colors."

She doesn't think for a minute that Hanna Andersson's success was all her own doing. "I certainly don't think I did this by myself. For one, my husband and I started this together. The good thing about our relationship was that we had completely different skills. I had the business background, and he was the creative one—he really created the catalog and the brand. But so many people we worked with contributed to making Hanna what it is today."

The list of factors that contributed to the success of Hanna Andersson is long. Denhart credits the complementary skills she and Tom brought to the enterprise; locating a vendor in Sweden that made fantastic cotton clothes; good timing as Baby Boomers were looking for high-quality clothing for their children; and plain old luck. And she gives a significant amount of credit to Hanna Andersson's employees: "We hired some people in the beginning who were just crucial to Hanna's success—you are so dependent on your employees. We always encouraged people to act like partners; you know, 'Please don't just do what we tell you to do. Give us ideas on how to do things better. Take the ball and run with it.'"

Denhart notes that one of the advantages of starting a business in the United States is the sheer size of the market, and the expansion of the Internet enabled Hanna Andersson to take advantage of that: "One thing that makes it so much easier in America than in my home country of Sweden is that the market is huge. You know, Hanna serves such a niche. You need a big market to support something like that. One language is a huge advantage. I mean, if you compare the EU with America, which is about the same-size market, it is certainly not as easy to get your products out [in the European Union]."

The Internet, a result of federally funded research (see "Reality Check: Building the Internet" earlier in this chapter), allowed Denhart to bring her niche product to scale in the large US market. As one marketing expert attests, "The Internet has opened up all sorts of niche marketing opportunities that either never existed before, or were too expensive to tap into."[92] Denhart recounts her story:

> We computerized really early on. . . . When we first started, we didn't have a computer, which was '83; but two years later we [did], for word processing and managing catalog orders. . . . I also had an older son who pushed me to get on the Internet. But we were really one of the first catalog companies to do this.
>
> It's a big cost saver for a mail-order company because instead of having people on the phone, taking orders, we actually have the customers do the work for us when they enter the order via the Internet. I am a big fan of the Internet. The Hanna website quickly became the preferred way for customers to place their orders.

Denhart lists other public investments that have helped provide a stable environment for her business to operate:

> For example, the electricity works, the sewer system works, the banking system has regulations so we can trust our banks. I actually wish we had *more* banking regulation. . . .
>
> If we didn't have a postal service that worked, our whole business model would have been impossible. . . . You know, there are

PHOTO COURTESY OF GUN DENHART

You need to pay taxes because you need to support the infrastructure in your society. You can't have a healthy business in an unhealthy community.

— GUN DENHART

countries where you can't rely on the mail. I mail a letter to my brother in Spain and it comes back three times over! How can you conduct business in a country where the mail doesn't work?

Denhart believes strongly in the importance of education, particularly early-childhood education, and argues that it should be a high priority of businesses. In 1999 she was a founding board member of the Oregon Business Association, which lobbies for progressive business issues like education and improved health care.

> For the long-term success of the state [Oregon], you need to make the education of your kids a priority. I strongly believe that you need to pay taxes because you need to support the infrastructure in your society. You can't have a healthy business in an unhealthy community.

Businesses really rely on an educated workforce and should be [willing to] spend money on public education. It's kind of a no-brainer to me. And it's [baffling] that we can have people arguing and saying, 'I don't have kids in public schools, so why should I care about public education?' And it's not only education: you need clean water; you need a safe society; you need protection from crime. It's so obvious to me I just get mad that it's an issue at all!

Finally, because Denhart believes strongly that her employees were a big part of the success of Hanna Andersson, when she and her husband sold the company in 2001 their appreciation for the role of their employees made the transition profoundly different from most sales. Although there was no contract requiring them to do so, the Denharts devised a formula for rewarding employees based on their salary and their length of service. "There was no way we were not going to give the employees a part of the proceeds. There was plenty of money to go around. And we didn't do this alone—a lot of people contributed to the success of the company."

With tears welling up and a lump in her throat, Denhart recalls meeting with each department about the sale of the company and thanking employees for their contributions. "There were so many tears all around," she recalls. "For some, the checks allowed them to pay off their debts. The less money they made, the more grateful they seemed to be for the bonus," she adds.

REALITY CHECK

Technical Innovation, Research, and Development

"Stories of the lone inventor and the garage genius are compelling. Ultimately, however, whether spun by history textbooks or proponents of laissez-faire economics, these stories are largely myth," reports the Breakthrough Institute. "Technologies ranging from rail transport to nuclear energy and from microchips to the Internet were all invented by government-supported researchers, developed with public funding or first deployed through government purchasing and incentives."[93]

According to economist Robert Kuttner, "Economic history since the industrial revolution strongly suggests that technical learning, not the process of perfect competition [between supply and demand], drives growth over time."[94] The free-market interplay of supply and demand is great at producing a set good at the best price, but real economic growth and progress are driven by innovation.

Basic research about the way the world works, a fundamental building block of innovation, is the result of the free flow of ideas and cannot be copyrighted.[95] No one can copyright the existence of gravity or the weight of an atom, only a book or piece of writing about it. As a result, there is little incentive for businesses to invest in such research. That's why Kent Hill argues, "societies will under-invest in basic research unless it is supported by government."[96]

Mapping the human genome is a clear example of such basic research. Funded through the National Institutes of Health (NIH) and the US Department of Energy, this groundbreaking project cost upward of $3 billion over 13 years.[97] Once the genome is mapped, anyone can take advantage of the newly discovered information to develop new medicines. This is the point where research shifts from "basic research" to "applied research" and, finally, to "product development."

Because specific technologies and ideas can be copyrighted or patented, there is notably more incentive for companies to invest in the product development end of the research spectrum. But even those investments are limited, as other companies will soon come out with competing products that eat into their margins. Additionally, some projects, like the creation of the Internet or the development of new energy technologies, require a scale of research and long-term commitment that is simply beyond the scope of any one company, necessitating governmental support.

Underlying these limitations is the market itself. Pure market economics is designed to squeeze out all the excess profit through the interplay of supply and demand, delivering the right amount of goods at the best possible price but leaving little to invest in long-term research or development. That is, supply and demand is concerned with the present moment. As such there is little concern for technical learning over time built into the economic model.[98]

Because research is so crucial to our long-term growth, and because there are so many disincentives for business to make such investments, we have historically relied on government to fund the bulk of basic research, along with some applied research and product development as well (the creation of the Internet is more akin to "product development" but on a grand, forward-looking scale).

Driven by the Cold War and the Space Race, federal funding of R&D reached its peak in 1964 at nearly 2 percent of gross domestic product (GDP).[99] While the federal share of R&D has been declining, government remains the primary funder of basic research while the private sector pays for most product development.[100] The budget proposal introduced in early 2011 by Congressman Paul Ryan would have cut federal science and technology R&D investments per capita by an additional 28 percent,[101] eroding one of the more important tools we have for fostering long-term economic growth and sustainability.

Abigail Disney: Government Creates a Fertile Ground for Business

Abigail Disney is a philanthropist, a filmmaker, and an heir to the Disney fortune.

Despite all of Abigail Disney's hard work and personal accomplishments, she acknowledges the significance of being born into wealth: "It's absolutely an accident of my birth. And that's sort of the point—that there shouldn't be dynasties built around the simple good luck of being born related to somebody very wealthy."[102] Nevertheless, luck is not the only factor she attributes to her success in her current philanthropic work: "I like to think I have been pretty effective in what I've done so far, but I haven't done it on my own. In order to do the work that I do, I rely on a tax code that supports a vigorous nonprofit sector."[103]

Abigail Disney is the granddaughter of Roy Disney, Walt Disney's brother and business partner, and an heir to the Disney fortune. She is a filmmaker and a philanthropist as well as the co-founder and the co-president of Daphne Foundation, a progressive social change foundation that makes grants to grassroots community-based organizations working with low-income communities in New York City.[104] Her documentary *Pray the Devil Back to Hell* won numerous awards, including Best Documentary at the Tribeca Film Festival.[105] The film chronicles the story of Christian and Muslim Liberian women who came together to pray for peace outside the Presidential Palace, a nonviolent protest credited with reinvigorating stalled peace talks.[106] Today she serves on the boards of the Roy Disney Family Foundation, the White House Project, the Global Fund for Women, and the Fund for the City of New York as well as the advisory boards of a broad range of organizations working in the areas of poverty, women's issues, education, and the environment.

As she readily points out, the Disney family fortune has greatly benefited from policies, both historically and currently, that have allowed the business to flourish and expand, making it one of the most well-known corporations in the world. She highlights social infrastructures that many others take for granted as being pivotal in the success of the Disney business. From the early days of the Walt Disney Company, her grandfather and great-uncle relied on federal protections after losing the rights to their first creation, Oswald the Lucky Rabbit, to their original distributor. Disney explains: "[My grandfather] soon registered a copyright on a new character named Mickey Mouse. It was 1928, and it was neither the first nor the last time the Walt Disney Company benefited from a federal system of protections, laws and taxes that created fertile ground for building a business empire."[107]

Government support of a positive business climate goes far beyond just copyright protection. She expands:

> My grandfather would be the first person to tell you that he managed to amass his fortune not in spite of but *because of* the American system. After all, without reliable and safe roads

there would be no such things as Disneyland; without high-functioning legal systems and a well-regulated business environment, there would have been no copyright protection for Mickey Mouse, no intellectual property protection for Snow White. And frankly, without a Marshall Plan, there would have been no European markets into which to expand, a move that permanently changed the Disney Company from a reasonably successful film company in the United States into a massive multinational corporation.[108]

Also worthy of note is the FCC, which regulates the airwaves that carried the *Disneyland* television series and *The Mickey Mouse Club.*

Disney clearly recognizes the importance of an efficiently operating government in the creation of individual wealth, and she translates her passion for that sentiment into advocating for progressive taxation and social responsibility. One of the issues about which Disney is most vocal is the need for a strong estate tax. "The estate tax is the cornerstone of a progressive system that leaves wealthy heirs with ample funds while providing the government with the resources it needs to build an environment for the common good. By preserving it, we not only restore billions in revenue to the national treasury—we also restore our most cherished collective ideals as a nation."[109]

Disney not only advocates that wealthy individuals ought to pay their fair share in taxes but also points out that her sector of business is made stronger by the support of taxpayer funds:

> I certainly never asked anyone to hand me anything I didn't earn, and I don't intend to try to compound my already good fortune by enjoying security, health, and good social order without contributing to the cost of those things by paying my fair share of taxes. . . .
>
> There is no question that the whole [nonprofit] sector is larger and stronger and more robust because of the many millions of

PHOTO BY ROBIN HOLLAND

Without high-functioning legal systems and a well-regulated business environment, there would have been no copyright protection for Mickey Mouse, no intellectual property protection for Snow White.

— ABIGAIL DISNEY

other dollars that flow into it because of the estate and other taxes. The loss of those millions upon millions would have a terrible impact on a sector already under enormous strains from the increase in demand and decrease in revenue caused by the difficult economic times we're in.[110]

Disney is a refreshing example of a prominent inheritor and successful business leader who vocally expresses that she and her family did not do it alone. She powerfully articulates the role of government in the success of both the Walt Disney Company and her own nonprofit sector while simultaneously promoting the need for a strong tax code to support such institutions through her philanthropic and activist work.

Jim Sherblom: Regulation Makes It a Fair and Open Game

As the CFO, Jim Sherblom guided one of the world's most successful biotech companies, Genzyme, through its crucial early years.[111]

Jim Sherblom worked in the biopharmaceutical industry for two decades. In the early 1980s, he was chief financial officer of Genzyme, one of the largest public biotech firms in the United States, with more than 1,700 employees. That might seem like enough for one career, but between 1989 and 1993 Sherblom was president and CEO of another biotech startup company called Transgenic Sciences Inc. Then he founded his own venture capital firm, investing in life science companies. For Sherblom the idea that anyone made their money alone, and so has no obligations, is patently ridiculous: "The opportunities to create that wealth are all taking advantage of public goods—like roads, transportation, markets—and public investments. None of us can claim it was all personal initiative. A piece of our success was built upon this infrastructure that we all have this inherent moral obligation to keep intact."

One of the examples of public benefits Sherblom lifts up is the tremendous liquidity and market stability provided by our system of financial regulation. In 1986 he oversaw the issue of Genzyme's initial public offering. The IPO was accompanied by a dramatic increase in the company's value, from $50 million at its last round of private financing to $500 million two years later as a public company. Says Sherblom, "When we were a private company at $50 million, investors had to be willing to keep their investment for several years. Only private equity investors and venture capitalists were willing to do that. Once you're in the public marketplace, you have much bigger pools of capital. A buyer could sell it the next day if they changed their mind. So they're willing to pay a substantial premium to reduce the risk of their investment in this way."

What is this liquidity worth? "My guess is that it's worth 30 to 50 percent of the value of these publicly traded companies," suggests Sherblom.

It's the fact that people feel comfortable and have liquidity—that they can trade in and out of them so easily.

More products have come out of the United States' biotech industry than all of the rest of the world's biotech industries combined, and I think it has something to do with the risk-taking culture of American business. These companies are going through $100 million before you even know if the drugs are going to work. So you have to be in a culture that is willing to pool lots of resources because they're bets that are too big for any one group to take.

But, he adds, the risk-taking pays off because the federal government steps in at key points. Take the case of Ceredase, Genzyme's initial blockbuster drug for the treatment of Gaucher's disease:

The original research that we were all basing the targeting of a protein around was all public domain. Our initial work was funded by the NIH, to see if it was feasible to produce a functional protein. Finally, when you have gone through and gotten FDA [US Food and Drug Administration] approval, you know you have some clear claims that you can make, and you are protected for a period of time from other people coming out and making similar claims for products they haven't done similar levels of testing on. We have one of the world's biggest and most innovative pharmaceutical industries because of the FDA.

The same is true in the investment world. I wish that all our firms were regulated at an appropriate level by the SEC because oftentimes people who are not SEC-regulated are doing things inside a black box that, if not outright illegal, are clearly unethical. There is no way of competing against them if they don't have to follow the law or even ethical behavior and can so grossly

misrepresent what they are doing. For those of us who are investors who care about how our money is made, who want to make
a good return but want to do it legally and ethically, having some
independent regulator who can force a certain transparency on
these black-box models is enormously helpful. It keeps the game
as a fair and open game, and everybody can have confidence in
the system.

Sherblom's view of his own career echoes his take on Genzyme's
success. Hard work and smart risk taking paid off, but so did breaks
at key moments—timing is everything:

There's no objective reality that suggests that people who went
to Harvard Business School with me and have had successful
careers—that that's purely an indication of their personal merit.
You look at any objective data and say, "OK, some of it's luck,
some of it's personal intelligence and capability, some of it's perseverance and willingness to take chances, and some of it is that
the industry emerges and for a time it's able to create X number
of people with really great opportunities." You have to catch that
particular wave with the right preparation for that wave.

My wife and I were both very good at what we set out to do and
very lucky to have been born at the time we were born. My kids
look at us and say, "From the early 1980s through the late 1990s,
the economy expanded in such a way that if you were willing to
work hard and you were educated, like Yale and Harvard, you
had opportunities to see your net worth increase 10-fold!" That's
not true today.

Now, says Sherblom, the economy we face is very different
from the one that rewarded him—and that makes the argument
for giving back even more urgent.

This Great Recession of 2008 is different from any other financial catastrophe that happened during my working career. We
are going to be a very different society with very different expectations about what is possible for a young, ambitious person
who wants to do well in their life. . . .

PHOTO COURTESY OF JIM SHERBLOM

None of us can claim it was all personal initiative. A piece of our success was built upon this infrastructure that we all have this inherent moral obligation to keep intact.

— JIM SHERBLOM

It may not be sustainable and it may be more painful if the richest 5 percent take the vast majority of the gains from here forward, and so you are pushing everyone else down further.

Elaborating on the 2008 financial collapse itself, Sherblom expresses deep appreciation for the role of government in stabilizing markets before even more damage was done:

I never would have guessed how much the government could become an underwriter of last resort. When you see the power in capitalism of creative destruction, you often don't talk about the downside of the destruction that is going on in people's lives. It's partly the government's fault that things got so out of hand by removing all of the regulations during the Clinton and the Bush years, but it's also clear to me that if they had pulled a Herbert Hoover and decided to just let it play itself out, which some of the advisers were suggesting, it would have taken us at least another generation to recover from the downturn.

The fact that almost all of the financial assets are close to if not already back at the values that they had before the downturn suggests that we rightly or wrongly had some pretty smart and courageous people at the helm as we went through that storm. And that's something that companies cannot individually do. They cannot trust each other in the middle of the storm. They have to have some independent actor who is trying to help pull things together. . . .

If I were to say, "How do we come out of this better for having lived through the experience?" it has to be that we put back in place those kinds of protection that allow each competitor to know that the other competitors are playing fairly.

After many years in the business world, Sherblom turned in a new direction. In 2004 he received his master's degree in divinity from Andover Newton Theological School and continued to work as a venture capitalist for a number of years, though he has now primarily wound down his venture capital work and focuses most of his time and energy on serving his Unitarian Universalist congregation.

I have been serving a [Unitarian Universalist] congregation in Brookline as their pastor, and there is a deep strain in American culture of communitarianism, believing that we ought to be looking out for each other, to love our neighbors as ourselves, and be the good Samaritan. Then there is this deep strand of individualism that everybody should do it on their own and the people who are falling out of the system must have done something wrong. I think you could get most Americans to affirm both of these views as being true, and yet they are deeply in conflict with each other.

We came into the twentieth century with a fairly dramatic fight between labor and capital. By the end of the twentieth century, it was clear that capital had won. Now the question is, OK, if capital is in the driver's seat, as it clearly is, how do you end up finding a reasonable balance so that people aren't taken advantage of on either side—so that those who are capital holders get a proportionate return from their capital while leaving enough incentive in the system so that everybody can have a living wage?

I don't think it's rocket science. It's not impossible to find that balance. For most of American history, we have found some reasonable balances in that regard, including the mid–twentieth century, the 1940s, '50s, '60s. I just think we are out of whack right now. We can't even have the conversation because people start hyperventilating when they hear that you would be taking anything away from the richest 5 percent. Somehow making sure that everyone has a living wage is un-American. It wasn't historically, but it is certainly how the debate is now crafted.

In discussing how these values are reflected in his personal life and outlook, Sherblom adds:

My wife and I both grew up working-class, so we didn't come with wealth from our parents. Our approach has always been to give back, to pay back a fair share for the infrastructure, and to know that everybody else is taken care of so that there is that safety net—that the people at the bottom really do have a living wage. If that ends up taking a third of our income, between various kinds or forms of taxes, that doesn't seem an unreasonable share for us to give back for living in a society that was structured such that we could make higher multiples from our good, hard efforts than we could in most other societies, which couldn't give us those kinds of opportunities and didn't have the infrastructure in place to let us find those successes. Our lives and our success are uniquely American.

CHAPTER 5

Policy Implications and the Public Investment Imperative

Shifting Perspectives and the Built-Together Reality

As has become clear throughout this book, the simplistic self-made myth of the past is woefully inadequate to describe reality. More importantly, it has a destructive impact on our public policy debates.

It is time that we talk about business success in a way that acknowledges and incorporates *all* its contributing factors. The built-together reality acknowledges a central truth overlooked by the self-made myth: We are not islands. Rather, our prosperity is deeply intertwined with the broader society around us. As Gun Denhart stated, "You can't have a healthy business in an unhealthy community." Every business, no matter how successful, is operating within a framework that was built by generations of public investments in the common good. That legacy in now part of what Peter Barnes calls the "commons," and it is at the heart of every business success story today.

The Entrepreneur's Role in Individual Success

There is a nugget of truth in the self-made story. That is, business leaders and entrepreneurs make groundbreaking innovations, take major risks, sacrifice short-term gratification, and exercise leadership in ways that rally the energies of many around them. In doing so, they help propel their business ventures forward down the road to success and, in many cases, strengthen the communities they serve in the process.

Many of the entrepreneurs and business leaders profiled in this book had great ideas or worked to fill an unmet need. Many brought a particular innovation or skill set to their work. And all have certainly worked hard and taken risks. Gun Denhart discovered and filled an unmet need for high-quality, colorful children's clothing, launching Hanna Andersson. Most readers of this book likely own a cell phone that uses some of the embedded software that Jerry Fiddler and the team at Wind River Systems developed. Nikhil Arora and his business partner Alejandro Velez at Back to the Roots found a great way to reuse waste coffee grounds and make money doing it. And how many of us have not sat down and enjoyed a pint of Ben & Jerry's ice cream, a pleasure made possible thanks to the joyful energy and inventiveness of Ben Cohen and his business partner, Jerry Greenfield?

From their stories we know they made great personal sacrifices, working long hours and taking very little pay, especially in the early years of their businesses. Many of the individuals profiled in this book also demonstrate great management skills and the leadership to rally large teams toward a single vision. They should be recognized for their leadership, innovation, hard work, and sacrifice. But to be fair, we should always remember that other factors contributed to their success as well.

Society's Role in Individual Success

As our economy has become more integrated, it has become even harder to separate the role of society from that of the individual. Even in the earliest days of our nation, when the self-made myth first emerged, there was a clear public role in supporting individual success that was often invisible to the very people who benefited from it. In the mythical image of the frontiersman and the farmers of our nation's youth, they carved their livelihoods out of the raw wilderness. Even that "wilderness," however, was provided through governmental action and the spoils of war with native peoples and the colonial powers in Europe. There has never been a time in our history when individual success was truly independent from the contributions of society or governmental action.

Try as we may, it is simply impossible to completely untangle the contributions of the individual from those of society in making individual success possible. The entrepreneurs and the business leaders profiled in this book have all benefited, both personally and in their business activities, from the investments and the structures made possible through governmental action. The personal testimonies of these successful individuals are a powerful rejection of the self-made myth in the United States.

If one expanded the pool of individuals profiled in this book, the stories would be much the same. On the personal side, they may have attended public schools, gone to college on the GI Bill, or benefited from our network of free public libraries. Their business most likely has used our public roads to ship its goods, the publicly created Internet to reach its customers, our public education system for educated workers, patent and copyright law to protect its intellectual property, and the rules and regulations of our market to bring confidence and predictability to its investors and customers.

In addition to the central role of government, there are nongovernmental actors that contribute to individual success. Images of community barn raisings come to mind as do the supports that many receive through our deep and rich network of nonprofit organizations. Even these nonprofit organizations, however, are supported in part by special provisions in the US tax code. Any comprehensive understanding of individual success must take these societal contributions into account.

Unequal Opportunity and Societal Barriers

The self-made myth has traction in part because we *want* to believe that those who are wealthy and successful in our nation are so because of their own hard work, risk taking, and leadership. Unfortunately, in addition to the role of society and government discussed above, individual success is also shaded by the societal effects of race and gender as well as the fortune of one's birth to a wealthy or not-so-wealthy family.

The self-made myth, for all its flaws, nonetheless reflects a vision of society that many wish to be true. That is, many of us believe that hard work and sacrifice should be the determining factors of one's fortune and wealth, not race, gender, or the circumstances of one's birth. It is the only way that significant differences in income and wealth can be reasonably justified. By that measure, though, our society has fallen far short. Many, many people work hard their entire lives and have little to show for it. Race, gender, class, birthright, and other factors still weigh heavily on one's prospects in life.

Although our nation's founding documents lifted up noble and aspirational phrases like "all men are created equal," it took nearly 100 years before slavery was abolished and another 100 years before Civil Rights victories cleared out the unjust Jim Crow laws of the South. And it will likely take decades, if not centuries, before discrimination based on race and gender in this country ceases to exist. Even though the story of the self-made man is a myth, we should not cease striving to create the conditions under which every American has a real opportunity to succeed in this world, free of the societal barriers that privilege some groups over others.

Historical Timing and Luck

In some ways the randomness of luck intersects with the randomness of race, gender, and birth to a wealthy family, for it is something that is beyond any of our control. We don't decide to be born Black, with a Y chromosome, or tall. Nor do we decide the relative wealth of the family into which we are born. Nonetheless this genetic lottery plays a profound role in who succeeds and who does not. There is an element of luck and timing, however, that is independent of the societal barriers discussed earlier.

John Paul Getty's comical axiom of success, "Rise early, work hard, and strike oil,"[1] referred to earlier in the text, captures this well. For every successful businessperson who rose early and worked hard, there are thousands of others who rose equally early and worked equally hard, but their work did not pay off with the same level of success due to factors beyond their control. An awareness of the randomness of luck should give us pause when we elevate some above others, as though their relative success and wealth is a measure of their work ethic, risk taking and inventiveness and somehow suggests a lack of effort on the part of others.

If random luck and the societal barriers of race, gender, and privilege do play a significant role in determining which hardworking early risers succeed and which do not, it casts serious doubt on any effort to rationalize economic inequality as simply the result of differing levels of "effort." It is not. As such there is just cause for reining in extreme inequality.

Historical timing is another form of luck for those born at the right time. Unlike true luck, however, timing is often a reflection of public policies of the era. Those who came of age during the economic boom of the 1950s and 1960s—when unions were strong and the federal government was making massive investments in the United States and its citizens—had significantly more economic opportunity (provided they were White and male) than those entering the workforce now, amidst the Great Recession and a significantly weakened public sector following 30 years of tax cutting for the wealthy.

Summary

The built-together reality provides a framework for thinking about the myriad factors that contribute to individual success. This more complete understanding has significant implications on how we view government, the public policies we formulate, and the public investments we make as a society.

A Note on the Role of Government

As is made clear throughout this book, government plays a key role in fostering an environment that supports individual success and the creation of wealth. We are not in fact islands but part of a community of individuals whose prosperity is deeply intertwined. Government plays a vital role that is overlooked, or in some cases outright ignored, by purveyors of the self-made myth.

Despite this crucial role, many pundits on the right have expended enormous energy and resources to diminish and demonize government in our society. As conservative activist Grover Norquist famously declared in 2001, "I don't want to abolish government. I simply want to reduce it to the size where I can drag it into the bathroom and drown it in the bathtub."² Their campaign to destroy public support for government has been so thorough and successful that the word *government* itself need only be attached to another and it drops like an anchor in the sea of public opinion. Case in point is the phrase *government health care,* or even the phrase *government schools,* which some on the right have begun using in place of *public schools.*³

To say that popular sentiment toward government is negative would be an understatement. If you ask people about specific things that government does, however, like educating the next generation, building and maintaining roads and vital infrastructure, protecting our air and water from polluters, and providing Medicare to seniors, their attitude changes dramatically. Poll after poll shows that while people often favor budget cuts in the abstract, they are against budget cuts when you start to get specific.[4] Perhaps this is simply because the anti-government rhetoric of recent years has been successful in diminishing the concept of government but not the things that government does. So what does government actually do? What has been the historic role of government in our society?

The first and most widely accepted role of government is ensuring our mutual security and protection. That basic instinct is a key reason why primitive people organized themselves into tribes long before there was government. The most visible examples of government acting as protector are of course national defense, followed by local police and fire departments. This vital role of protector also extends to consumer safety standards, building inspections, worker safety, environmental protections, civil rights, and more. It includes the protection of intellectual property, copyright and patent enforcement, mediating contract disputes, and ensuring fair rules of the road.

The second major role of government—a role that has become increasingly important in our modern, interdependent economy— is laying the foundation for our shared prosperity and strengthening the public infrastructure upon which we all rely. Government builds and maintains roads, ports, schools, parks, and other public spaces. Government invests heavily in scientific research and the development of cutting-edge technologies. Government also invests in people and strengthening our middle class through programs such as the GI Bill, student loans, food assistance, and Social Security.

In carrying out these two roles—government as protector and government as investor in our shared prosperity—government ends up filling a significant third role: consumer. In building a school, government is investing in future generations, but it is also acting as a consumer by buying building supplies and the labor of plumbers, electricians, and construction workers. As a result, money collected through taxes is not taken out of the economy but rather moved from one part of the economy to another to achieve goals that we as citizens deem important. As an added bonus, tax dollars used to invest in and achieve our shared goals have a far greater economic stimulus, or bang for the buck, than do tax cuts.[5]

Whether acting as protector of our mutual security or investing in our shared well-being, when functioning properly, government is serving all of its citizens. As such its primary allegiance should not be just to the wealthy elite in our society but to the young and old, worker and owner, low-income and high-income. Some believe, for good reason, that government is currently beholden to powerful financial interests. We do not disagree. The Supreme Court's 2010 decision in *Citizens United v. Federal Election Commission*—allowing unlimited corporate spending on political broadcasts to influence elections[6]—coupled with enormous concentrations of wealth in the hands of a few has only made matters worse by allowing a small group of well-heeled individuals and corporations to buy government favors.

If, as we assert in this book, government lays the foundation of economic prosperity, what do these individuals gain by demonizing the very government on which their businesses rely? By creating the impression that their wealth and prosperity is entirely their own doing, they can shirk any responsibility to pay for those investments, and in doing so pass the responsibility off to others. By ignoring the contributions of their employees to their own success, they can justify their extravagant CEO salaries while suppressing efforts of others to secure a fair living wage.

Of course, not all business leaders and entrepreneurs deny society's contributions to their success. By making the invisible visible and by recognizing the self-made myth for what it is, we can take measure of the public policy choices before us with clear eyes.

Tax Policies for the Built-Together Reality

A Progressive Income Tax

Most of the individuals profiled in this book talk about recognizing the enormous benefits of working in US society and the desire to give back. This includes both charitable contributions to institutions that build opportunity but also tax dollars that provide vital public goods, services, and education for those who are coming up behind them. They know that charity is not a substitute for a well-functioning government. Instead of a deep resentment toward the "tax man," there is a recognition by these individuals that they are part of a larger society and that, in the end, we are all in this together.

But giving back is not a matter of benevolence; it's a responsibility. By acknowledging the role that government plays in strengthening the wide array of public investments and the economic framework upon which business success is possible, it follows that they should contribute toward the maintenance of those shared assets. The man whom many consider to be the father of our free-market economic system, Adam Smith, once wrote: "The subjects of every state ought to contribute towards the support of the government, as nearly as possible, in proportion to their respective abilities; that is, in proportion to the revenue which they respectively enjoy under the protection of the state."[7]

Put more directly, those who receive the greatest benefit from the economy our government makes possible should contribute the greatest share toward its maintenance. Viewed this way, progressive tax policies are not about "punishing success," as some have asserted, but rather about giving back to support the society that makes one's success possible. Smith goes even further to state: "It is not very unreasonable that the rich should contribute to the public expense, not only in proportion to their revenue, but something more than in proportion."[8]

Many of the business leaders profiled in this book have spoken out in support of such progressive tax policies. In fact, there has been a growing chorus of high-wealth individuals and successful business leaders who are calling for higher taxes on themselves, including ending the Bush tax cuts for high-income earners.

Many of these leaders have also taken it a step further by calling for a new top-tier income tax for those earning more than $1 million. Such a plan was put forth by Representative Jan Schakowsky, with new rates starting from 45 percent for those earning more than $1 million per year up to 49 percent for those earning over $1 billion. Schakowsky's bill would also eliminate the special tax break for capital gains and dividends,[9] which Warren Buffett wrote about in his August 14, 2011, *New York Times* op-ed, "Stop Coddling the Super-Rich."[10]

At the state level, those who understand the built-together reality have called on states to meet their budget shortfalls by enacting new top-tier income tax brackets as has been done in Connecticut and New York (New York's top-tier brackets were a temporary, two-year measure that has not yet been renewed as of the date of this writing).[11]

Ending the Special Tax Break for Capital Gains and Dividend Income

Our current system of taxing income earned from wealth at a much lower rate than income earned from work is an affront to the idea that work should be rewarded. It is the special tax break for capital gains and dividend income that Warren Buffett is highlighting when he complains that he pays a lower tax rate than do the people who work for him.

Under current law, investment income from capital gains and dividends, where most of Buffet's income comes from, is taxed at a much lower rate than income derived from work. The top marginal income tax rate for income earned from wages is 35 percent (on joint taxable income over $373,650).[12] By comparison, the top tax rate for income earned from long-term capital gains and dividends, even for individuals whose income puts them in the 35 percent tax bracket otherwise, is only 15 percent. As a result, a surgeon earning $400,000 will pay a top marginal rate of 35 percent while a wealthy heir sitting on a boat collecting $400,000 in investment income pays a top rate of only 15 percent.[13]

At the very least, we should ensure that income earned from accumulated wealth is taxed at the same rate as income earned from the actual labor of one's hands and mind—income from work. The "People's Budget" from the Congressional Progressive Caucus does this by taxing investment income as ordinary income.[14] Even the Deficit Commission convened by President Obama recommended taxing investment income as ordinary income in its final recommendation.[15] The Buffet Rule in the deficit plan presented by President Obama in late 2011 would partially address this by requiring that millionaires pay at least the same tax rate as do middle-class Americans.[16]

Taxing Inherited Wealth

Once we acknowledge that the wealth of those most fortunate among us is not entirely self-made, that society and the public investments made possible through governmental action also played a major role, it is just and fair to ask that a portion of that wealth be returned to society. Nineteenth-century industrialist Andrew Carnegie articulated this sentiment long before the estate tax was ever created: "It is difficult to understand why, at the death of its possessor, great wealth . . . should not be shared by the community which has been the most potent cause or partner in its creation . . . under a just system of taxation."[17]

But it's more than just giving back, because concentrated wealth passed along from generation to generation has the capacity to destroy the very fabric of our nation. We founded this nation in part to escape the aristocracies of old Europe, where a person's fortune had more to do with one's family bloodlines than the hard work one is willing to exert in life. As noted earlier, even though the self-made man is a myth, that does not mean we should cease striving to create the conditions under which a person's fortune is a reflection of his or her own hard work. Limiting inherited wealth is central to moving us closer to that reality.

A large and growing chorus of high-wealth individuals recognize this reality and have spoken out in favor of a strong estate tax. More than 2,000 wealthy individuals have signed United for a Fair Economy's "Call to Preserve the Estate Tax." Many of the individuals profiled in this book, including Jerry Fiddler and Abigail Disney, have spoken out in favor of the estate tax.[18] In September 2010, Robert Rubin, former Treasury secretary and co-chairman at Goldman Sachs, joined with Fortune 400 member Julian Robertson in penning an op-ed in the *Wall Street Journal* calling for the preservation of the estate tax.[19] John C. Bogle, founder of the Vanguard Group, has spoken out in favor of the estate tax, as well.[20] And perhaps the two most prominent and vocal advocates for a strong estate tax are Bill Gates Sr.[21] and Warren Buffett.[22]

As of this writing, the estate tax is levied at a rate of 35 percent after the first $5 million in net assets are exempted ($10 million for a couple). At that level a single child of a married couple can inherit more, tax free, than the average American earns in four lifetimes.[23] United for a Fair Economy and Responsible Wealth believe that this is far too generous. We support the estate tax bill introduced by Senator Bernie Sanders, which would establish a $3.5 million exemption, after which a graduated estate tax would apply with rates beginning at 45 percent, rising to a top rate of 65 percent for estates exceeding $500 million ($1 billion for a couple).[24]

Ensuring That Corporations Pay Their Fair Share

On the campaign trail in 2011, presidential candidate Mitt Romney declared in response to a protestor, "Corporations are people, my friend."[25] Well, they sure don't pay taxes like people do. Bank of America, Boeing, Citicorp, Exxon/Mobil, and GE paid no corporate income taxes in 2010.[26]

It's not just a matter of a few isolated tax dodgers, either. Total corporate income taxes have steadily fallen over the past several decades. In 1952 corporate income taxes accounted for roughly 30 percent of federal revenue. That has fallen to less than 10 percent today.[27] This, despite the fact that their wealth and financial success is made possible by the roads, ports, courts, education system, and publicly funded research that is paid for and supported by our tax dollars. In short, the built-together reality applies to corporations too.

These corporations have a responsibility to help support the public infrastructure and society that makes their wealth possible. That means closing corporate tax loopholes, including overseas tax havens, that have been used by corporate tax accountants in an elaborate shell game to hide their profits.[28] It means ending subsidies to established industries like Big Oil, as has been proposed by President Obama in his 2011 jobs plan.[29]

Investing in America and Paying It Forward

Rebuilding America's Infrastructure

As noted previously, the built-together reality and the public investment imperative are as old as the nation itself, though by other names. George Washington's first address to the new Congress lifted up the need to develop an infrastructure to connect the new nation.[30] This was followed by large-scale investments in ports, rail, and roads. Later we as a nation invested in public education at all levels: land-grant colleges, libraries, a postal system, and much more. In the second half of the twentieth century, we saw the construction of the Interstate Highway System, massive federal investment in technological innovation, and the creation of the Internet. These investments helped build a foundation upon which entrepreneurship and business success are possible.

Many of the business leaders and entrepreneurs featured herein speak to the role of those investments in making their business possible. It's hard to imagine where Anirvan Chatterjee and his Bookfinder.com venture would be were it not for the public investments in creating the Internet. Similarly, the Interstate Highway System dramatically reduced the cost and the time required to ship goods across the nation, with huge ripple effects across the economy. Mass-transit systems enable employers like Glynn Lloyd to draw from a larger pool of potential employees. Many of the examples in this book echo the positive impacts that result when we come together as a nation to make needed investments that strengthen the economic and societal foundation upon which we all stand.

In preparing our nation for a twenty-first-century economy where globalization and sustainability are factored in, a new type of investment is in order. Wise investment in public education, from pre-K through higher ed, is essential, but so are publicly funded research into new technologies and building a new generation of public infrastructure like high-speed rail, mass transit, and an alternative-energy grid. Such an investment strategy will sow the seeds of prosperity for the next generation.

In addition to providing entrepreneurs with a solid infrastructure upon which to build their businesses over the long term, such investments can help jump-start our ailing economy at a time when jobs are sorely needed across the county. Mark Zandi of Moody's Analytics estimates that every dollar we invest in public infrastructure generates $1.59 in economic stimulus.[31] As any businessperson would tell you, that is a very wise investment.

Among other things, the American Recovery and Reinvestment Act enacted in February 2009 sought to rebuild our nation's deteriorating infrastructure while providing much-needed jobs. It has clearly had a significant impact. In the second quarter of 2011, the Congressional Budget Office estimated that ARRA has increased GDP by between 0.8 and 2.5 percent, increased the number of full-time-equivalent jobs by 1.4 to 4 million, and lowered the unemployment rate by 0.5 to 1.6 percentage points.[32] Without ARRA we may well be looking at a double-digit unemployment rate and a far worse recession than we currently face.

Many have called for a second economic stimulus or a jobs plan to pick up where ARRA left off. Such an effort, done right, has the potential not only of helping Americans still struggling amid the Great Recession but also of laying the foundation for our long-term prosperity as a nation.

Investing in Opportunity for All Americans

Many of the individuals profiled in this book attest to how they personally benefited from investments in individual opportunity. Martin Rothenberg speaks of receiving an education under the GI Bill. Kim Jordan notes the Pell Grants that helped her pay for college. Anirvan Chatterjee, Nikhil Arora, and Jerry Fiddler speak of publicly supported education in general and the nation's many land-grant universities.

Education—or, more to the point, the availability of high-quality education to all regardless of income and family background—is an important tool for increasing social mobility. According to a paper from Princeton University and the Brookings Institution, "Improving educational opportunity is the classic way to increase mobility. A society with a weak education system will, by definition, be one in which the advantages of class or family background loom large. We need to ensure that children from less advantaged backgrounds have the same educational opportunities as those whose parents can afford to enroll them in nursery school at an early age, live in a high-priced neighborhood with good schools, and send their children to college."[33]

If we are serious about promoting a society in which persons of modest means can rise up and start successful businesses of their own, we must ensure that education is not just the privilege of those from affluent backgrounds. That begins with a well-funded pre-K program that gives families from low-income backgrounds a leg up. That investment must go through K–12 on up to the college and university level.

Finally, it's not enough to have high-quality universities. Those universities must be available to all Americans regardless of income. Offering more students loans is not enough. As noted earlier, graduating a generation of students saddled with debt stifles entrepreneurship. Instead we should beef up funding for Pell Grants and similar subsidies for low- and middle-income households. At the same time, we should be increasing taxpayer support for higher education to lessen, and even turn back, years of tuition hikes that have made a college education unaffordable to many.

Finally, we should increase the resources available for the Small Business Administration to provide training and support for newly emerging businesses as well as loan guarantees for start-up businesses, especially women- and minority-owned businesses that find it more difficult to get a traditional bank loan.

Social Safety Nets and an Economic Floor

There are many reasons to invest in social safety nets and an economic floor that relate in part to our common humanity and understanding that we are all in this together but also to a deeper understanding of individual wealth and success. As the built-together reality suggests, the success and good fortune of one over another often has little to do with how hard one worked. When people lose their jobs from a plant closing, it is not a measure of their personal character but rather the misfortune of economic forces far bigger then themselves. To allow them to spiral down the economic ladder is not only unjust but has negative consequences for society as a whole.

At the same time, there is an argument that social safety nets help increase social mobility. As noted earlier, there is evidence that safety nets, including health care, food and nutrition programs, and unemployment insurance, increase social mobility by enabling people to weather crises and eventually break out of poverty.

Finally, by providing a floor to ensure that everyone's basic needs are met, strong social safety nets may actually increase entrepreneurship. One fact that may surprise many readers is that Europe, with its much more expansive welfare state and universal health care, has a much higher rate of small business ownership than does the United States. Only about 7 percent of Americans are self-employed compared with 9 percent of French, 12 percent of Germans, and 26 percent of Italians. Even when measured by small (fewer than 20 employees) and medium-sized (fewer than 500 employees) firms, the United States is at or near last among Organisation for Economic Co-operation and Development nations (most European nations, Canada, the United States, and a few others).[34]

Observing this fact, Dean Baker writes, "One possible explanation for the relatively smaller role of small business in the US economy is that concern over access to health insurance makes many people reluctant to strike out on their own and start a small business. The prospect of being stuck without health insurance has to be very scary for a 50-year-old with some health problems."[35] Put another way, entrepreneurship is a risky venture. But if the consequences of failure are too severe, such as the loss of health care, entrepreneurship can be stifled.

Ensuring That the Framework of the Economy Is Fair

Ensure Fair "Rules of the Road"

Like the piano wires that suspend actors in old kung fu movies,[36] our economy cannot function without the unseen rules and regulations that ensure the smooth operation of business, including copyright protections, property rights enforcement, contract resolution, disclosure requirements, and consumer protections of various types. The rules that govern worker safety and the quality of our air and water are also vital to the functioning of our economic system. In the wake of the 2008 financial crisis, the need for solid financial and consumer regulation is more evident than ever.

Many of the individuals profiled in this book speak in compelling ways about the importance of this stabilizing framework. Jim Sherblom, Peter Barnes, and Amy Domini all speak to the importance of well-regulated financial markets. Domini also found ways to use in her business model the data collected by various agencies regarding environmental and worker safety. Glynn Lloyd speaks of the importance of food-safety standards in providing confidence to the system. Others, including Abigail Disney, tell compelling stories of our court system's role in protecting intellectual property.

Our nation would be well served by toning down the anti-regulation rhetoric. The question is not whether we should regulate—*we must.* The questions we should ask are whether those regulations are adequate to meet our changing economic reality and whether they are enforced fairly across all businesses. To do so means we need *more* funding for regulatory agencies, not less, because spotty enforcement from an underresourced agency is likely to result in uneven, and thus unfair, enforcement. For example, speaking from the perspective of a relatively small fish in her industry, Domini knows that she gets more firsthand scrutiny from regulators than do the big mutual funds because they don't have the regulators to handle the big ones.[37]

Ensure That Workers Share in the Prosperity

As noted earlier, Henry Ford made waves when he began paying his workers double the prevailing wage to reduce turnover and ensure that his workers could afford to buy the very cars they were making.[38] Ensuring that workers share in the productivity gains they make possible is not just about benevolence or generosity; it's a sound economic principle that has been documented by economists. That is, when the middle class is strong, the economy as a whole does well. As Jean Gordon, whom we quoted in the introduction, said, "The best way to help small businesses like ours is to put more money in the hands of the middle class who will spend the money as customers of our businesses."[39]

Although slashing wages and employee benefits may give a business a competitive edge over its competitors in the short term, when all businesses begin doing it the entire middle class can be wiped out or significantly weakened. That's why broadly enforced minimum-wage and living-wage laws work. It's not harmful to a business to pay its employees a fair wage so long as its competitors are doing the same. And the economy as a whole does better when they do.

Some of the business leaders we've interviewed take this commitment to heart. King Arthur Flour[40] and New Belgium Brewing,[41] for example, have strong employee ownership policies. Others, like Seventh Generation and Whole Foods, limit CEO pay to a multiple of their lowest-paid employee's wages. Ben & Jerry's had similar CEO pay ratios in its earlier years, as did furniture maker Herman Miller.

As important as the efforts of these socially responsible businesses are, real change must be systemic in nature and broadly applied to all businesses. As such there has been a growing movement to curb extravagant CEO salaries. The Institute for Policy Studies estimates the CEO-to-worker pay ratio in 2010 to be 325-to-1.[42] Recent legislation included within the financial reform bill requires a biannual nonbinding up-or-down shareholder vote on CEO salary packages at large publicly traded companies,[43] a policy that Responsible Wealth members helped promote through shareholder resolutions. While this represents progress, more work must be done.

Progress in ensuring that workers share in the wealth they helped create has been equally mixed. As of July 2009, the federal minimum wage was increased to $7.25,[44] which is still significantly less than its peak in 1968, when it was more than $10 per hour in 2010 dollars.[45] Fortunately, 18 states have a minimum wage that is higher than the federal minimum wage. Additionally, by 2007 at least 130 cities had living-wage ordinances.[46] This is clearly progress, but more should be done to ensure that all whose work contributes to the creation of wealth, from the shop floor to the sales floor to the top floor, share in the prosperity.

Ensure That Equal Opportunity Really Is Equal Opportunity

Throughout our history Americans have worked to make sure that the creed *All men are created equal* rings true in our nation. In doing so we want to know that a person's fortune is, to the greatest extent possible, the result of hard work, not skin color, gender, or any head start received in life. There is clear evidence, however, that race and gender do still matter, as do a host of other factors that have nothing to do with a person's ability.

We must remain vigilant in our enforcement of anti-discrimination laws and continue with affirmative action programs. We should also invest in programs that help broaden opportunity and break down the intergenerational class divisions in society, including those drawn along the lines of race. That means investing in early-childhood education, well-funded K–12, and additional Pell Grant funding for low-income students. It also means investing in microenterprise and small-business loan programs to help those with great ideas—even if they don't come from a family with wealth—turn those ideas into the next great business venture.

Wealth, unlike income, provides the security and the startup capital one needs to start a business. Yet Blacks hold only 10 cents of net wealth, and Latinos hold only 12 cents to every dollar White families hold.[47] By comparison, Blacks earn 59 cents and Latinos earn 57 cents to every dollar Whites earn of median family income.[48] One reason why the wealth disparity is so much greater than the income disparity is because wealth, unlike income, can be transferred from one generation to the next through inheritance and gifts. Without substantial wealth few Blacks and Latinos have the startup capital to start their own business. This is one reason why SBA business loans for minority and women entrepreneurs, including the one that helped Thelma Kidd start her successful bookstore chain, are so important.

A number of the individuals profiled herein attribute at least part of their success to the role that government played in undoing some of the societal barriers of the past. In addition to Thelma Kidd, Amy Domini noted the lawsuit at another brokerage firm that opened up the industry to female brokers like herself. Similar policies helped other entrepreneurs, like Glynn Lloyd, overcome the societal barriers of race. By ensuring that everyone has an opportunity to build a successful business, such policies open the door to more small businesses and a more vibrant economy.

A Call to Action

Using Your Voice

Because the self-made myth is so pervasive in our public dialogues today, it is necessary that we fight it at all levels. Each of us, from line workers to students to corporate CEOs, has a role in debunking the myth and its corrosive impact on the public policy debates of our times. But we can't just knock down the self-made myth. We must also lift up in its place a more honest and complete understanding of individual and business success—what we call the built-together reality.

If you are a business leader, owner, or CEO, you have a unique position of credibility to challenge the self-made myth as it applies to your own life and success.

- When you see a letter or editorial in your local newspaper about how some state or national progressive tax policy "punishes success," write a letter back, pointing out that you are a successful businessperson but that your success is not entirely your own doing. Think about how the stories in this book apply to your own life, and tell your story of success and how it was supported by an array of public investments and fair rules made possible through governmental action. Explain why you believe you have an obligation to help support those public structures through a progressive tax system.

■ If you are active in a local Chamber or business association, be vocal at meetings about the need to fund, through our tax system, vital infrastructure that builds a foundation of prosperity that undergirds the entire community, including the businesses that operate within it.

■ Share your story with others through Responsible Wealth. We are gathering additional written and video testimonials like the ones in this book, and we welcome your story. To learn more see "About Responsible Wealth" at the back of this book.

If you are a progressive activist or community leader, challenge those in your group who may instinctively, and mistakenly, assume that all business leaders are against you. Some are, but many others are not. Seek out the business leaders in your community with an open mind and foster cross-class alliances that build greater political power and, ultimately, help better all of our communities. When you see local business leaders speaking out in favor of funding important public services, let them know they are not alone. Applaud their leadership and build new relationships where you can.

If you are an elected official, you have a unique opportunity to frame the kinds of policies we advocate in chapter 5, using language that moves toward a deeper understanding of the origins of individual and business success. As we move the public debate, it is essential that we advance this more honest narrative, including the built-together reality and the importance of investing in the common good, that is, the public investment imperative. To do so we need voices at every level, including those of elected officials who are allies in this cause.

If you are a student or an academic, organize programs at your university and use this book as part of class curricula, especially if you are at one of the universities that is now teaching Ayn Rand's *Atlas Shrugged* as part of its curriculum. As part of this book release, we will be touring the country and organizing panel discussions featuring some of the businesspeople profiled herein as well as other business leaders who share this view. If you want to use this book for a class or similar project, contact Berrett-Koehler for bulk pricing.

And for everyone interested in fostering a more honest dialogue about individual and business success, find an organization in your community that is taking action for a more fair economy. Help ensure that it is doing more than fighting for the short-term policy win but also working to change the way people think about wealth creation in the process. There are thousands of such local groups across the nation—far too many to list here. That said, United for a Fair Economy currently works with state-level organizations in 24 states as part of our Tax Fairness Organizing Collaborative (TFOC); these organizations are working to advance progressive tax policy at a state level, and all would welcome more supporters. UFE also has a national network of supporters engaged in online activism and community education. To learn more about the TFOC or UFE's national network, see "About United for a Fair Economy" at the back of this book.

Responsible Wealth in Action

In 2001 Bill Gates Sr., a successful lawyer in Seattle, Washington—and father of the Microsoft founder by the same name—overheard a conversation in an elevator, where one man said to another, "We're very close to getting rid of the estate tax." He later said it hit him like a ton of bricks that the country would even *consider* repealing our only tax on accumulated wealth.[1]

Soon thereafter Gates happened to be seated next to a member of the Rockefeller family at a philanthropy conference, and he mentioned that if he had more time, he'd start an organization called something like Wealthy People in Favor of an Estate Tax. As luck would have it, his dinner companion was able to tell him, "There's already a group doing it, called Responsible Wealth, and I'm a member."

Mr. Gates sent us an e-mail, got engaged, and began what has been 10 years of advocacy alongside Responsible Wealth and our parent organization, United for a Fair Economy, to preserve a strong estate tax. This work started with an ad in the *New York Times* and went on to include lobby days, personal meetings with senators, numerous press conferences, a book on the subject (and a book tour), and speaking engagements across the country. Gates's advocacy, speaking with authority as a seasoned attorney and as the father of a rather successful entrepreneur, has been one of the most important factors in preventing the repeal of the estate tax.

There are many more success stories that we could tell from Responsible Wealth's 14-year history, like Charles Demeré's standing up at our founding conference in 1997 and pledging to give away his capital gains tax cut (inspiring our Tax Fairness Pledge); Barry Hermanson, founder of Hermanson's Employment Service, who led a successful campaign for a living wage in San Francisco; Judy Wicks, who converted her restaurant to paying every employee a living wage in response to our Living Wage campaign; and the 90-plus New Yorkers who signed an open letter to the governor in 2009, saying "raise our taxes" to help fill the $19 billion budget gap. We could go on with this list for a long while.

In the three years prior to this book's publication, much of the work of UFE and Responsible Wealth has focused on the critical tax debate in Washington, as the Bush tax cuts, originally set to expire in 2010, were extended through 2012. Throughout this debate Responsible Wealth members have spoken in favor of preserving a strong estate tax, ending the Bush tax cuts for high-income earners, and ending special tax breaks for unearned income. So many wealthy individuals were speaking up that Ashlea Ebeling of *Forbes* magazine wrote:

It's not just billionaires like Warren Buffett and Bill Gates who say that there should be an estate tax, but just plain old rich folks are speaking out too.

More than 2,000 wealthy Americans who have paid or expect to owe estate taxes have signed a call to preserve the estate tax that was put out by United for a Fair Economy's Responsible Wealth project. The signers include professors, farmers, small business owners, and lawyers . . . Some signers have a few million dollars, others tens of millions, but they are united in the words of the call: "We believe that permanent repeal of the estate tax would be bad for our democracy, our economy, and our society."

The signers of the Responsible Wealth estate tax call are not just outliers, and some are billionaires. They include Forbes 400 members David E. Shaw, Julian Robertson Jr., George Soros, John Sperling, and Ted Turner. All six children of David Rockefeller, the oldest Forbes 400 member, have signed too.[2]

Warren Buffett pushed this one step further in August 2011 in his powerful op-ed "Stop Coddling the Super-Rich."[3] This article helped jump-start the public debate about the need for a more progressive tax system that did not exempt those at the very top from paying their fair share. His leadership contributed to President Obama's including the "Buffett Rule," which would require that millionaires pay at least the same tax rate as middle class Americans, in the deficit reduction plan he proposed in September 2011.[4]

And while Buffett's leadership, and that of other super-wealthy individuals, is admirable, we must always ensure that new faces and new voices enter the debate and strengthen the call for fairer and more responsible policies. That is the challenge we face, and it is part of the reason why we wrote this book. If we are to truly shift the public debate, we must ensure that as the *Forbes* writer noted, "It's not just billionaires like Warren Buffett and Bill Gates." It can't be, not if we want to have a real impact.

Thank you for joining us in this important dialogue.

Notes

Introduction: Public Policy and the Success Narrative

1. "Final Score" with David Asman, *Fox Business*, interview with Brian Miller recorded on July 8, 2011.

2. Barry Goldwater, *The Conscience of a Conservative* (Kentucky: Victor, 1960), 61.

3. Harriet McLeod, "Texas Governor Rick Perry Launches Presidential Bid," Reuters, August 13, 2011, http://www.reuters.com/article/2011/08/14/us-usa -politics-perry-idUSTRE77C1EI20110814 (accessed October 28, 2011).

4. "Mitt Romney Remarks: August 11, 2011," C-SPAN Video Library, http:// www.c-spanvideo.org/program/Romneya (accessed October 28, 2011).

5. Avi Feller and Chad Stone, "Top 1 Percent of Americans Reaped Two-Thirds of Income Gains in Last Economic Expansion; Income Concentration in 2007 Was at Highest Level Since 1928, New Analysis Shows," Center on Budget and Policy Priorities, September 9, 2009, http://www.cbpp.org/cms/index .cfm?fa=view&id=2908 (accessed October 28, 2011).

6. Bryan Thomas, "Intel to Acquire Wind River Systems for Approximately $884 Million," Wind River, June 4, 2009, http://www.windriver.com/news/ press/pr.html?ID=6921 (accessed October 28, 2011).

7. "Estate Tax Speaker: Jerry Fiddler," United for a Fair Economy, http://fair economy.org/estate_tax_teleconference_nov_2010/jerry_fiddler (accessed October 28, 2011).

8. "Estate Tax Speaker: Jean Gordon," United for a Fair Economy, http://fair economy.org/estate_tax_teleconference_nov_2010/jean_gordon (accessed October 28, 2011).

9. Robert Reich, "The Truth about the American Economy," Reader Supported News, May 31, 2011, http://readersupportednews.org/opinion2/279-82/6108 -the-truth-about-the-american-economy (accessed October 28, 2011).

10. Janet Lowe, *Warren Buffett Speaks: Wit and Wisdom from the World's Greatest Investor* (New York: John Wiley & Sons, 1997), 164–65.

Chapter 1: *The Self-Made Myth*

1. Robert Kuttner, *Everything for Sale: The Virtues and Limits of Markets* (Chicago: University of Chicago Press, 1996), 211.

2. Rmuse, "American Pariah: Why the Founding Fathers Would Reject the GOP," Politicus USA, November 21, 2010, http://www.politicususa.com/en/american-pariah-why-the-founding-fathers-would-reject-the-gop (accessed October 28, 2011).

3. "Selected Short Stories of Mark Twain," Le Moyne, http://lemoyne.edu/FacultyStaff/CelebratingMarkTwain/TwainReadings/tabid/2006/Default.aspx (accessed October 28, 2011).

4. "Gimme a Break! Mark Twain Lampoons the Horatio Alger Myth," History Matters, http://historymatters.gmu.edu/d/4935 (accessed October 28, 2011).

5. "The Story of the Good Little Boy Who Did Not Prosper," The Galaxy, http://www.twainquotes.com/Galaxy/187005f.html (accessed October 28, 2011).

6. See note 3 above.

7. Irvin Wyllie, *The Self-Made Man in America: The Myth of Rags to Riches* (New Brunswick: Rutgers University Press, 1954), 16.

8. Phineas T. Barnum, *Art of Money Getting* (Bedford, MA: Applewood Books, 1999), 5.

9. "Teaching with Documents: The Homestead Act of 1862," National Archives, http://www.archives.gov/education/lessons/homestead-act (accessed October 28, 2011).

10. Malcolm Gladwell, *Outliers: The Story of Success* (New York: Little, Brown, 2008), 61–62.

11. Wyllie, *Self-Made Man,* 24.

12. Ibid.

13. Yuval Elmelech, *Transmitting Inequality: Wealth and the American Family* (Lanham, MD: Rowman & Littlefield, 2008), 71.

14. Wyllie, *Self-Made Man,* 109–10.

15. Ibid., 172.

16. Sarah Stanwick and Peter Stanwick, "Sunbeam Corporation: 'Chainsaw Al' and the Quest for a Turnaround," Auburn University, http://www.auburn .edu/~stanwsd/sunbeam.html (accessed October 28, 2011).

17. Sam Pizzigati, *Greed and Good: Understanding and Overcoming the Inequality that Limits Our Lives* (New York: Apex Press, 2004), 54.

18. Scott Klinger, "The Bigger They Come, The Harder They Fall: High CEO Pay and the Effect on Long-Term Stock Prices," United for a Fair Economy, April 6, 2001, http://www.faireconomy.org/files/pdf/Bigger_They_Come.pdf (accessed October 28, 2011).

19. Jennifer Reingold, "Executive Pay," *Bloomberg Businessweek*, April 17, 2000, http://www.businessweek.com/careers/content/jan1990/b3677014.htm (accessed October 28, 2011).

20. Frank Cocozzelli, "Paul Ryan Borrows a Page from Ayn Rand's 'Morality,'" Roosevelt Institute, http://www.rooseveltinstitute.org/new-roosevelt/paul -ryan-borrows-page-ayn-rand-s-morality (accessed October 28, 2011).

21. Stephen Moore, "'Atlas Shrugged': From Fiction to Fact in 52 Years," *Wall Street Journal*, January 9, 2009, http://online.wsj.com/article/NA_WSJ_PUB: SB123146363567166677.html (accessed October 28, 2011).

22. Eric Sapp, "GOP Must Choose: Ayn Rand or Jesus," American Values Network, May 27, 2011, http://americanvaluesnetwork.org/2011/05/gop-must-choose -ayn-rand-or-jesus (accessed October 28, 2011).

23. "The Smallest Minority on Earth," *The Rush Limbaugh Show*, March 31, 2009, http://www.rushlimbaugh.com/home/daily/site_033109/content/01125110 .guest.html (accessed October 28, 2011).

24. Vladimir Shlapentokh, "How Is Elitist Ayn Rand a Tea Party Hero? The Contradiction Should Concern America," *Christian Science Monitor*, October 14, 2010, http://www.csmonitor.com/Commentary/Opinion/2010/1014/How -is-elitist-Ayn-Rand-a-tea-party-hero-The-contradiction-should-concern -America (accessed October 28, 2011).

25. Seth Lubove and Oliver Staley, "Schools Find Ayn Rand Can't Be Shrugged as Donors Build Courses" *Bloomberg*, May 5, 2011, http://www.bloomberg.com/ news/2011-05-05/schools-find-ayn-rand-can-t-be-shrugged-as-donors-build -courses.html (accessed October 28, 2011).

26. Ibid.

27. Yaron Brook, "'Atlas Shrugged' Sets a New Record," Ayn Rand Institute, Janu- ary 21, 2010, http://www.aynrand.org/site/News2?page=NewsArticle&id=24817 (accessed October 28, 2011).

28. Ernesto Tinajero, "Tales of Two Capitalisms: Ayn Rand vs. Horatio Alger," Sojournes, February 5, 2010, http://blog.sojo.net/2010/02/05/tales-of-two -capitalisms-ayn-rand-vs-horatio-alger (accessed October 28, 2011).

29. Ibid.

30. House Republican Conference Press Office, "Hensarling Joins American Job Creators, House Republicans for Interactive Forum on Job Creation," GOP .gov, March 16, 2011, http://www.gop.gov/press-release/11/03/16/hensarling -joins-american-job-creators (accessed October 28, 2011).

31. John Parkinson, "Dead on Arrival? Congress Divided on Obama's Plan to Raise Taxes," ABC News, September 19, 2011, http://abcnews.go.com/blogs/ politics/2011/09/congress-divided-on-presidents-deficit-reduction-plan (accessed October 28, 2011).

32. "Editorial: How Big Gov't Strangles the Job Creators," Investors.com, June 24, 2011, http://www.investors.com/NewsAndAnalysis/Article/576448/ 201106241829/Small-Business-And-Big-Govt.aspx (accessed October 28, 2011).

33. Daniel J. Mitchell, "Abolish the 'Death Tax,'" Cato Institute, April 23, 2009, http://www.cato.org/pub_display.php?pub_id=10143 (accessed October 28, 2011).

34. Harlon L. Dalton, *Racial Healing: Confronting the Fear between Blacks and Whites* (New York: Double Day, 1995), 128.

35. Michael Moore, "Face It, You'll Never Be Rich," Znet, October 9, 2003, http:// www.zcommunications.org/face-it-youll-never-be-rich-by-michael-moore (accessed October 28, 2011).

Chapter 2: Busting the Myth

1. Suzanne Mettler, "Reconstituting the Submerged State: The Challenge of Social Policy Reform in the Obama Era," *Perspectives on Politics* 8, no. 3 (2010), http://journals.cambridge.org/action/displayFulltext?type=6&fid=7 874753&jid=PPS&volumeId=8&issueId=&aid=7874752&fulltextType=RA& fileId=S1537592710002045 (accessed October 28, 2011).

2. Sara Robinson, "The Myth of the Self-Made American: Why Progressives Get No Respect," Campaign for America's Future, October 29, 2010, http:// www.ourfuture.org/blog-entry/2010104329/myth-self-made-american-why -progressives-get-no-respect (accessed October 28, 2011).

3. Gwendolyn Parker, "George W. Bush's Secret of Success," *New York Times*, May 28, 1999.

4. See note 2 above.

5. "Donald Trump Profile," *Forbes,* May 2011, http://www.forbes.com/profile/donald-trump (accessed October 28, 2011).

6. "The Trump Organization," Funding Universe, http://www.fundinguniverse.com/company-histories/The-Trump-Organization-Company-History.html (accessed October 28, 2011).

7. Robert Halasz and A. Woodward, "The Trump Organization," CBS Interactive, http://findarticles.com/p/articles/mi_gx5202/is_1993/ai_n19122300/?tag=mantle_skin;content (accessed October 28, 2011).

8. "The Trump Organization, Inc." *Bloomberg Businessweek,* http://investing.businessweek.com/research/stocks/private/snapshot.asp?privcapId=344985 (accessed October 28, 2011).

9. See note 6 above.

10. "The Trump Organization—Resurgence: 1994–97," International Directory of Company Histories, http://www.enotes.com/company-histories/trump-organization/resurgence-1994-97 (accessed October 28, 2011).

11. "Donald Trump on Government Reform," On the Issues, http://www.ontheissues.org/Celeb/Donald_Trump_Government_Reform.htm (accessed October 28, 2011).

12. "Trump Abuses Eminent Domain," Club for Growth, April 19, 2011, http://www.clubforgrowth.org/perm/pr/?postID=893 (accessed October, 28 2011).

13. "*Casino Reinvestment Development Authority v. Coking:* The Abuse of Eminent Domain in Atlantic City," Institute for Justice, http://www.ij.org/component/content/article/37-privatepropertyrights/1002-casino-reinvestment-development-authority-v-coking (accessed October 28, 2011).

14. "Donald Trump @ CPAC 2011," YouTube, http://www.youtube.com/watch?v=PlT9fAkjoXU (accessed October 28, 2011).

15. David Seaman, "Donald Trump: Obama Has Blown It; I'm Going to Announce My Decision about Running for President in June," *Business Insider,* December 22, 2010, http://www.businessinsider.com/donald-trump-my-economic-policies-would-vary-greatly-from-obamas-2010-12#ixzz1TQfh6W8E (accessed October 28, 2011).

16. "The Political Fray," CNN All Politics, 1996, http://www.cnn.com/ALLPOLITICS/1996/conventions/long.beach/perot/political.fray.shtml (accessed October 28, 2011).

17. "Reform Party History," PBS, August 10, 2000, http://www.pbs.org/newshour/bb/politics/july-dec00/reform_history.html (accessed October 28, 2011).

18. "Henry Ross Perot," *Forbes*, March 2011, http://www.forbes.com/profile/henry-ross-perot-sr (accessed October 28, 2011).

19. Ibid.

20. Gerald Posner, *Citizen Perot: His Life and Times* (New York: Random House, 1996), 10

21. Ibid., 14.

22. Ibid., 28.

23. Ibid., 26–33.

24. Ibid., 35.

25. Ibid., 38–39

26. Ibid., 34.

27. Ibid., 39.

28. Ibid., 46.

29. Ibid., 39.

30. Ibid., 41.

31. Ibid., 47

32. Doron P. Levin, "G.M. vs. Ross Perot: Breaking Up Is Hard to Do," *New York Times Magazine*, March 26, 1989, http://www.nytimes.com/1989/03/26/magazine/gm-vs-ross-perot-breaking-up-is-hard-to-do.html?src=pm (accessed October 28, 2011).

33. Andrew Vanacore, "Perot Systems: Dell Buys Ross Perot's Company for $3.9 Billion," *Huffington Post*, September 21, 2009, http://www.huffingtonpost.com/2009/09/21/perot-systems-dell-buys_1_n_293201.html (accessed October 28, 2011).

34. See note 18 above.

35. "Mobility Decreasing in Recent Decades," State of Working America, http://www.stateofworkingamerica.org/charts/view/228 (accessed October 28, 2011).

36. "The United States Produces Less Mobility than Many of Its International Peers," State of Working America, http://www.stateofworkingamerica.org/charts/view/233 (accessed October 28, 2011).

37. Richard Wilkinson and Kate Pickett, *The Spirit Level: Why Greater Equality Makes Societies Stronger* (New York: Bloomsbury Press, 2009), 159.

38. "Inequality, Mobility, NDD Spending, and the American Dream," On the Economy, September 10, 2011, http://jaredbernsteinblog.com/inequality

-mobility-ndd-spending-and-the-american-dream (accessed October 28, 2011).

39. Emily Beller and Michael Hout, "Intergenerational Social Mobility: The United States in Comparative Perspective," *The Future of Children* 16 (fall 2006), http://futureofchildren.org/futureofchildren/publications/docs/16_02_02. pdf (accessed October 28, 2011).

40. See note 38 above.

41. Avi Feller and Chad Stone, "Top 1 Percent of Americans Reaped Two-Thirds of Income Gains in Last Economic Expansion; Income Concentration in 2007 Was at Highest Level Since 1928, New Analysis Shows," Center on Budget and Policy Priorities, September 9, 2009, http://www.cbpp.org/cms/index .cfm?fa=view&id=2908 (accessed October 28, 2011).

42. Jane Mayer, "Covert Operations: The Billionaire Brothers Who Are Waging a War against Obama," *The New Yorker,* August 30, 2010, http://www.new yorker.com/reporting/2010/08/30/100830fa_fact_mayer#ixzz1Yg0AUGGZ (accessed October 28, 2011).

43. Ibid.

44. Yasha Levine, "7 Ways the Koch Bros. Benefit from Corporate Welfare," The Exiled Online, September 4, 2010, http://exiledonline.com/a-people-history -of-koch-industries-part-ii-libertarian-billionaires-charles-and-david-koch -are-closetcase-subsidy-kings-who-milk-big-government-tyranny-but-want -to-slash-spending-on-anyone-else (accessed October 28, 2011).

45. Ibid.

46. Ibid.

47. Bob Williams and Kevin Bogardus, "Koch's Low Profile Belies Political Power," Center for Public Integrity, July 15, 2004 (updated March 31, 2006), http:// projects.publicintegrity.org/oil/report.aspx?aid=347 (accessed October 28, 2011).

48. See note 42 above.

49. Sarah Owen, "David Koch Gives President Obama Zero Credit for Bin Laden's Death," New York Magazine Online, May 5, 2011, http://nymag.com/daily/ intel/2011/05/billionaire_conservative_david.html (accessed October 28, 2011).

50. See note 44 above.

51. See note 42 above.

52. Ibid.

53. Ibid.

54. Aili McConnon and Lawrence Delevingne, "Feeling Pinched, Some US Philanthropists Give More," *Bloomberg Businessweek*, November 25, 2008, http://www.businessweek.com/magazine/content/08_49/b4111054030529 .htm (accessed October 28, 2011).

55. Ibid.

56. Joshua Holland, "Ayn Rand Railed against Government Benefits, but Grabbed Social Security and Medicare When She Needed Them," AlterNet, http:// www.alternet.org/teaparty/149721/ayn_rand_railed_against_government _benefits,_but_grabbed_social_security_and_medicare_when_she_needed _them (accessed October 28, 2011).

Chapter 3: *The Built-Together Reality of Individual Success*

1. Malcolm Gladwell, *Outliers: The Story of Success* (New York: Little, Brown), 74.

2. Ibid.

3. Ibid., 131–32.

4. Ibid., 64–68.

5. Dave Kellogg, "Rise Early, Work Hard, and Strike Oil," Kellblog, December 10, 2008, http://kellblog.com/2008/12/10/rise-early-work-hard-and-strike-oil (accessed October 28, 2011).

6. "Success as Mere Luck," *Literary Digest* (1929), 9, as cited in Irvin Wyllie, *The Self-Made Man in America: The Myth of Rags to Riches* (New Brunswick: Rutgers University Press, 1954), 157.

7. Alden Whitman, "J. Paul Getty Dead at 83: Amassed Billions from Oil," New York Times Learning Network, June 6, 1976, http://www.nytimes.com/ learning/general/onthisday/bday/1215.html (accessed October 28, 2011).

8. Gladwell, *Outliers*, 111–12.

9. Dalton Conley, *Being Black, Living in the Red: Race, Wealth, and Social Policy in America* (Berkeley: University of California Press, 2009), 49–53.

10. United for a Fair Economy, "Born on Third Base: The Sources of Wealth of the 1997 Forbes 400" (Boston: United for a Fair Economy, 1997).

11. Sam Pizzigati, *Greed and Good: Understanding and Overcoming the Inequality that Limits Our Lives* (New York: Apex Press, 2004) 89.

12. Mazher Ali, Jeannette Huezo, Brian Miller, Wanjiku Mwangi, and Mike Prokosch, *State of the Dream 2011: Austerity for Whom?* (Boston: United

for a Fair Economy, 2011), 3, http://www.faireconomy.org/files/State_of_the
_Dream_2011.pdf (accessed October 28, 2011).

13. Jennifer Wang, "Mixed Signals: The State of Black Entrepreneurship,"
    Entrepreneur.com, March 9, 2009, http://www.entrepreneur.com/starting
    abusiness/article200506.html (accessed October 28, 2011).

14. Ibid.

15. Sylvia Allegretto and Steven Pitts, "The State of Black Workers before the
    Great Recession," UC Berkley Labor Center, July 23, 2010, http://laborcenter
    .berkeley.edu/blackworkers/blackworkers_prerecession10.pdf (accessed
    October 28, 2011).

16. Cathy Keen, "Workplace Rewards Tall People with Money, Respect, UF
    Study Shows," University of Florida News, October 16, 2003, http://news.ufl
    .edu/2003/10/16/heightsalary (accessed October 28, 2011).

17. Robert G. Lynch, *Rethinking Growth Strategies: How State and Local Taxes
    and Services Affect Economic Development* (Washington, DC: Economic Policy
    Institute, 2004), vii.

18. John F. Sargent Jr., "Federal Research and Development Funding: FY2011,"
    June 10, 2011, Congressional Research Service, http://www.ieeeusa.org/policy/
    eyeonwashington/2011/documents/rdfunding.pdf (accessed November 14,
    2011).

19. Robert Kuttner, *Everything for Sale: The Virtues and Limits of Markets*
    (Chicago: University of Chicago Press, 1996), 214.

20. Helen Aki, Zachary Arnold, Genevieve Bennett, et al., "Case Studies in
    American Innovation," December 2010, Breakthrough Institute, http://
    thebreakthrough.org/blog/Case%20Studies%20in%20American%20Inno
    vation%20report.pdf (accessed October 28, 2011).

21. Ibid., 17.

22. Human Genome Project Information, US Department of Energy Office of
    Science, http://www.ornl.gov/sci/techresources/Human_Genome/home
    .shtml (accessed October 28, 2011).

23. John W. Kendrick, Lester C. Thurow, Edward F. Denison, et al., "The Decline
    in Productivity Growth," Federal Reserve Bank of Boston, June 1980, www
    .bos.frb.org/economic/conf/conf22/conf22.pdf (accessed October 28, 2011).

24. Ha-Joon Chang, *23 Things They Don't Tell You about Capitalism* (New York:
    Bloomsbury Press, 2010), 3–6.

25. Abigail Disney, "Mickey Mouse, the Estate Tax and Me," *USA Today,* August 30, 2010, http://www.usatoday.com/news/opinion/forum/2010-08-31-column31 _ST_N.htm (accessed October 28, 2011).

26. Robert Reich, "The Truth about the American Economy," *Salon,* May 31, 2001, http://www.salon.com/news/politics/war_room/2011/05/31/the_truth_about _the_american_economy (accessed October 28, 2011).

27. Garrett Gruener, "I'm Rich; Tax Me More," *Los Angeles Times,* September 20, 2010, http://articles.latimes.com/2010/sep/20/opinion/la-oe-gruener-tax-the -rich-20100920 (accessed October 28, 2011).

28. John F. Witte, *The Politics and Development of the Federal Income Tax* (Madison: University of Wisconsin Press, 1985), 100.

29. Albert Einstein, "The World as I See It," American Institute of Physics, http:// www.aip.org/history/einstein/essay.htm (accessed October 28, 2011).

Chapter 4: Stories of Success and the Common Good

1. Irvin Wyllie, *The Self-Made Man in America: The Myth of Rags to Riches* (New Brunswick: Rutgers University Press, 1954), 119–20.

2. Mike Lapham interviewed Jerry Fiddler on September 11, 2003, and July 21, 2011. Unless otherwise specified, all subsequent information was obtained from those interviews.

3. Mike Lapham interviewed Glynn Lloyd on July 25, 2011. Unless otherwise specified, all subsequent information was obtained from that interview.

4. "FDA History—Part I," US Food and Drug Administration, http://www .fda.gov/AboutFDA/WhatWeDo/History/Origin/ucm054819.htm (accessed October 29, 2011).

5. George Washington, State of the Union Address 1790, January 8, 1790, InfoPlease, http://www.infoplease.com/t/hist/state-of-the-union/1.html# ixzz1Q74LcPOs (accessed October 28, 2011).

6. Ibid.

7. Robert Kutner, *Everything for Sale: The Virtues and Limits of Markets* (Chicago: University of Chicago Press, 1996), 211.

8. Louis M. Hacker, *Major Documents in American Economic History,* Volume I (Princeton: Van Nostrand, 1961), 89.

9. Lee Mertz, "Origins of the Interstate," US Department of Transportation, http://www.fhwa.dot.gov/infrastructure/origin.pdf (accessed October 28, 2011).

10. "Interstate Highway FAQ," US Department of Transportation, http://www .fhwa.dot.gov/interstate/faq.htm#question6 (accessed October 28, 2011).

11. Wendell Cox and Jean Love, "40 Years of the US Interstate Highway System: An Analysis," The Public Purpose, http://www.publicpurpose.com/freeway1. htm#econ (accessed October 28, 2011).

12. Abigail Disney, "Mickey Mouse, the Estate Tax and Me," *USA Today*, August 30, 2010, http://www.usatoday.com/news/opinion/forum/2010-08-31-column31 _ST_N.htm (accessed October 28, 2011).

13. Judy Pigott, "I'm a Genetic Lottery Winner—Tax Me!" Other Words, October 25, 2010, http://www.otherwords.org/articles/im_a_genetic_lottery _winner-tax_me (accessed October 28, 2011).

14. Mike Lapham interviewed Amy Domini on July 6, 2011.

15. "Estate Tax Speaker: John Russell," United for a Fair Economy, http://fair economy.org/issues/estate_tax/estate_tax_teleconference_november_2010/ estate_tax_speaker_john_russell (accessed October 28, 2011).

16. "Recovery Act Projects—Funds Obligated," US Department of Transportation, October 21, 2011, http://www.dot.gov/recovery/resources/totalfunds.pdf (accessed October 28, 2011).

17. "High-Speed Intercity Passenger Rail Program," US Department of Transportation, http://www.fra.dot.gov/rpd/passenger/2243.shtml (accessed October 28, 2011).

18. Brian Miller interviewed Thelma Kidd on August 9, 2011. Unless otherwise specified, all subsequent information was obtained from that interview.

19. "Slaton, TX Weather," IDcide—Local Information Data Server, http://www .idcide.com/weather/tx/slaton.htm (accessed October 28, 2011).

20. Julie R. Weeks, "Support for Women's Enterprise in the United States: Lessons Learned," National Association of Women Business Owners, http://www .nawbo.org/content_7845.cfm (accessed October 28, 2011).

21. "Warren Buffett," *Forbes*, March 2011, http://www.forbes.com/profile/warren -buffett (accessed October 28, 2011).

22. Janet Lowe, *Warren Buffett Speaks: Wit and Wisdom from the World's Greatest Investor* (New York: John Wiley & Sons, 1997), 164.

23. Ibid.

24. Vahan Janjigian, "Warren Buffett's Tax Fetish," *Forbes,* May 1, 2008, http://www .forbes.com/2008/05/01/buffett-vahan-janjigian-pf-ii-in_ty_0430soapbox _inl.html (accessed October 28, 2011).

25. Todd A. Finkle, "Warren E. Buffett and Berkshire Hathaway Inc.," Bnet, http://findarticles.com/p/articles/mi_qa5452/is_201005/ai_n56445240 (accessed October 28, 2011).

26. Yi-Hsin Chang, "Getting to Know Warren," The Motley Fool, April 29, 1999, http://www.fool.com/specials/1999/sp990429Berkshire002.htm (accessed October 28, 2011).

27. Bill Freehling, "Buffett 101: What Does Berkshire Hathaway Own?" Examiner.com, July 18, 2009, http://www.examiner.com/warren-buffett-in-national/buffett-101-what-does-berkshire-hathaway-own (accessed October 28, 2011).

28. Larry Kanter, "Warren Buffett," *Salon*, August 31, 1999, http://www.salon.com/people/bc/1999/08/31/buffett (accessed October 28, 2011).

29. Lowe, *Warren Buffett Speaks*, 165.

30. Tom Bawden, "Buffett Blasts System That Lets Him Pay Less Than Secretary," *Times* (London), June 28, 2007, http://www.timesonline.co.uk/tol/money/tax/article1996735.ece (accessed July 27, 2011).

31. Lowe, *Warren Buffett Speaks*, 168.

32. Warren Buffett, "Stop Coddling the Super-Rich," *New York Times,* August 14, 2011, http://www.nytimes.com/2011/08/15/opinion/stop-coddling-the-super-rich.html (accessed October 28, 2011).

33. Juliann Neher, "Warren Buffett Tells ABC Rich People Should Pay Higher Taxes," *Bloomberg,* November 21, 2010, http://www.bloomberg.com/news/2010-11-21/warren-buffett-tells-abc-rich-people-should-pay-more-in-taxes.html (accessed October 28, 2011).

34. Kevin Drawbaugh, "Buffett Backs Estate Tax, Decries Wealth Gap," Reuters, November 14, 2007, http://www.reuters.com/article/2007/11/14/us-buffett-congress-idUSN1442383020071114 (accessed October 28, 2011).

35. Warren Buffett, "My Philanthropic Pledge," CNN, June 16, 2010, http://money.cnn.com/2010/06/15/news/newsmakers/Warren_Buffett_Pledge_Letter.fortune (accessed October 28, 2011).

36. Mike Lapham interviewed Martin Rothenberg on September 25, 2003, and July 12, 2011. Unless otherwise specified, all subsequent information was obtained from those interviews.

37. Robert M. Berdhahl, "The Privatization of Public Universities," UC Berkeley, http://cio.chance.berkeley.edu/chancellor/sp/privatization.htm (accessed October 28, 2011).

38. "Transcript of Morrill Act (1862)," Our Documents, http://www.ourdocuments
.gov/doc.php?flash=true&doc=33&page=transcript (accessed October 28,
2011).

39. National Association of State Universities and Land-Grant Colleges, "The
Land-Grant Tradition," Association of State Universities and Land-Grant
Colleges, http://www.aplu.org/document.doc?id=780 (accessed October 28,
2011).

40. "The GI Bill's History," US Department of Veterans Affairs, http://www.gibill
.va.gov/benefits/history_timeline/index.html (accessed October 28, 2011).

41. "Tuition and Fee and Room and Board Charges over Time," Trends in College
Pricing 2010, College Board Advocacy and Policy Center, http://trends
.collegeboard.org/college_pricing/report_findings/indicator/Tuition_and
_Fee_and_Room_and_Board_Charges_Over_Time (accessed October 4,
2011).

42. Ibid.

43. "Institutional Revenues: Public Appropriations over Time," Trends in College
Pricing 2010, College Board Advocacy and Policy Center, http://trends
.collegeboard.org/college_pricing/report_findings/indicator/Institutional
_Revenues_Public_Appropriations (accessed October 4, 2011).

44. Ibid.

45. "Pell Grant Amounts," Trends in Student Aid 2010, College Board Advocacy
and Policy Center, http://trends.collegeboard.org/student_aid/report
_findings/indicator/accessible/Pell_Grants (accessed October 4, 2011).

46. Ibid.

47. "The American Recovery and Reinvestment Act of 2009: Saving and Creating
Jobs and Reforming Education," US Department of Education, March 7, 2009,
http://www2.ed.gov/policy/gen/leg/recovery/implementation.html (accessed
October 29, 2011).

48. "Federal Pell Grants," National Education Association, http://www.nea.org/
assets/docs/Federal_Pell_Grants_Chart_FY1976-2012.pdf (accessed October 29, 2010).

49. "Federal Loans: Percentage Borrowing, Number of Borrowers and Amounts,"
Trends in Student Aid 2010, http://trends.collegeboard.org/student_aid/
report_findings/indicator/Federal_Loans_Percentage_Borrwing_Number
_of_Borrowers_and_Amounts (accessed October 4, 2011).

50. Brian Miller interviewed Kim Jordan on August 30, 2011. Unless otherwise
specified, all subsequent information was obtained from that interview.

51. "Our Story," New Belgium Brewing, http://www.newbelgium.com/culture/our-story.aspx (accessed October 29, 2011).

52. "The Ten Biggest US Craft Breweries," CNBC, http://www.cnbc.com/id/39233398/The_10_Biggest_US_Craft_Breweries?slide=9 (accessed October 29, 2011).

53. "Welcome to the DDA," Downtown Development Authority, http://www.downtownfortcollins.org (accessed September 29, 2011).

54. "2010 Year in Review," Downtown Development Authority, http://www.downtownfortcollins.org/docs/year-in-review2010.pdf (accessed September 29, 2011).

55. "State Funding: A Historical Perspective," University of Colorado, https://www.cu.edu/content/timeline0 (accessed September 29, 2011).

56. Mike Lapham interviewed Anirvan Chatterjee on July 14, 2011. Unless otherwise specified, all subsequent information was obtained from that interview.

57. "Internet History," Computer History Museum, http://www.computerhistory.org/internet_history/index.html (accessed October 29, 2011).

58. Barry M. Leiner, Vinton G. Cerf, David D. Clark, et al., "Histories of the Internet," Internet Society, http://www.isoc.org/internet/history/brief.shtml (accessed October 29, 2011).

59. "About the National Science Foundation," National Science Foundation, http://www.nsf.gov/about (accessed October 29, 2011).

60. Walt Howe, "An Anecdotal History of the People and Communities That Brought about the Internet and the Web," A Brief History of the Internet, http://www.walthowe.com/navnet/history.html (accessed October 28, 2011).

61. Ibid.

62. Lauren DuBois, "IIA Commends FCC's Focus on Expanding High-Speed Internet to Rural America, Achieving Universal Broadband," Business Wire, http://www.businesswire.com/news/home/20110624005754/en/IIA-Commends-FCC%E2%80%99s-Focus-Expanding-High-Speed-Internet (accessed October 29, 2011).

63. Ibid.

64. Chuck Collins interviewed Peter Barnes on October 15, 2003. Mike Lapham interviewed Barnes on July 6, 2011. Unless otherwise specified, all subsequent information was obtained from those interviews.

65. Peter Barnes, "Capitalism, the Commons and Divine Right," E. F. Schumacher Society, http://www.smallisbeautiful.org/publications/barnes_03.html (accessed October 29, 2011).

66. Peter Barnes, *Who Owns the Sky?: Our Common Assets and the Future of Capitalism* (Washington, DC: Island Press, 2001), 118.

67. Chuck Collins, "Financial Markets as Commons," On the Commons, http://onthecommons.org/financial-markets-commons (accessed October 29, 2011).

68. Carol Graham, Robert E. Litan, and Sandip Sukhtankar, "Cooking the Books: The Cost to the Economy," Brookings Institution, http://www.brookings.edu/papers/2002/08business_graham.aspx (accessed October 29, 2011).

69. Tomales Bay Institute, *The State of the Commons,* Tomales Bay Institute, 2003, http://onthecommons.org/sites/default/files/stateofthecommons.pdf (accessed October 29, 2011).

70. Scott Klinger interviewed Amy Domini on December 23, 2003. Mike Lapham interviewed Domini on July 6, 2011. Unless otherwise specified, all subsequent information was obtained from those interviews.

71. "The Domini Story," Domini Social Investments, http://www.domini.com/about-domini/The-Domini-Story/index.htm (accessed October 29, 2011).

72. Dan DiBartolomeo and Lloyd Kurtz. "Managing Risk Exposures of Socially Screened Portfolios." *Northfield Working Paper,* 1999, http://www.northinfo.com/documents/63.pdf (accessed October 29, 2011).

73. "History of U.S. Stock Market Crashes," Market Volume, http://www.marketvolume.com/info/stock_market_crashes.asp (accessed October 29, 2011).

74. "The Investor's Advocate: How the SEC Protects Investors, Maintains Market Integrity, and Facilitates Capital Formation," US Securities and Exchange Commission, http://www.sec.gov/about/whatwedo.shtml (accessed October 29, 2011).

75. "Glass-Steagall Act—Further Readings," JRank, http://law.jrank.org/pages/7165/Glass-Steagall-Act.html (accessed October 29, 2011).

76. Doug Short, "A Complete Look at the History of Recessions in America," Business Insider, September 21, 2010, http://articles.businessinsider.com/2010-09-21/markets/30089410_1_recession-nber-official-end-date (accessed October 29, 2011).

77. "What Was the Glass-Steagall Act?" Investopedia, July 15, 2003, http://www.investopedia.com/articles/03/071603.asp#axzz1YhaiU42U (accessed October 29, 2011).

78. Binyamin Applebaum and David M. Herszenhorn, "Financial Overhaul Signals Shift on Deregulation," *New York Times,* July 15, 2010, http://www.nytimes.com/2010/07/16/business/16regulate.html?pagewanted=all (accessed October 29, 2011).

79. Chuck Collins interviewed Jim Sherblom on December 12, 2003, and March 23, 2010. Mike Lapham interviewed Sherblom on July 18, 2011.

80. Brian Miller interviewed Nikhil Arora on July 22, 2011. Unless otherwise specified, all subsequent information was obtained from that interview.

81. "From Bankers to Mushroom Farmers," Back to the Roots, http://www.backtotheroots.com/our-story (accessed October 29, 2011).

82. "2010 Innovation Award Winners," Social Venture Network, http://www.svn.org/index.cfm?pageId=1119 (accessed October 29, 2011).

83. Sarah Stankorb, "10 Generation Next Entrepreneurs to Watch," CNN Money, July 7, 2011 http://money.cnn.com/galleries/2011/smallbusiness/1107/gallery.generation_next_entrepreneurs/3.html (accessed October 29, 2011).

84. "Alejandro Velez and Nikhil Arora—The Courage to Ask," YouTube, http://www.youtube.com/watch?v=C4qtfgrTwLc&feature=player_embedded%20and%20http://nikhilarora.com/ (accessed on October 29, 2011).

85. Ibid.

86. "OBDC Small Business Finance: History," OBDC, http://www.obdc.com/index.php?option=com_content&view=article&id=22%3Ahistory-&catid=5&Itemid=7 (accessed October 29, 2011).

87. "The San Francisco Jobs Now Program," Human Services Agency of San Francisco, http://www.sfhsa.org/asset/Home/PrivateandNPEmployers InfoPacketupdated090409.pdf (accessed October 29, 2011).

88. Mike Lapham interviewed Ben Cohen on October 2, 2003, and July 19, 2011. Unless otherwise specified, all subsequent information was obtained from those interviews.

89. Constance L. Hays, "Ben & Jerry's to Unilever, with Attitude," *New York Times,* April 13, 2000, http://www.nytimes.com/2000/04/13/business/ben-jerry-s-to-unilever-with-attitude.html?pagewanted=all&src=pm (accessed October 29, 2011).

90. "Public Policy," B Lab, http://www.bcorporation.net/publicpolicy (accessed October 29, 2011).

91. Mike Lapham interviewed Gun Denhart on January 8, 2004, and July 13, 2011. Unless otherwise specified, all subsequent information was obtained from those interviews.

92. Noel Peebles, "12 Reasons Why a Business without an Online Presence Is Missing Out on a Goldmine of Potential Customers," Pandecta, http://www.pandecta.com/online-presence.html (accessed October 29, 2011).

93. "Case Studies in American Innovation," Breakthrough Institute, April 2009, http://thebreakthrough.org/blog/Case%20Studies%20in%20American%20Innovation.pdf (accessed October 29, 2011).

94. Kuttner, *Everything for Sale*, 192.

95. "Ask an Astrophysicist," NASA, September 8, 1996, http://imagine.gsfc.nasa.gov/docs/ask_astro/answers/960908.html (accessed October 29, 2011).

96. Kent Hill, *Universities in the US National Innovation System* (Tempe: Arizona State University, 2006), 6, https://wpcarey.asu.edu/seidman/reports/innovation.pdf (accessed October 29, 2011).

97. Human Genome Project Information, Human Genome Project Budget, US Department of Energy Office of Science, http://www.ornl.gov/sci/techresources/Human_Genome/project/budget.shtml (accessed October 29, 2011).

98. Kuttner, *Everything for Sale*, 191.

99. See note 96 above.

100. Ibid.

101. Adam Hersh and Sara Ayres, "Disinvesting in America: The House Republican Budget Plan in Action," Center for American Progress, April 14, 2011, http://www.americanprogress.org/issues/2011/04/disinvesting_america.html (accessed October 29, 2011).

102. Yuki Noguchi, "Showdown over Bush Cuts Revives Estate Tax Fight," NPR, September 11, 2010, http://www.npr.org/templates/story/story.php?storyId=129756032 (accessed October 29, 2010).

103. National press teleconference hosted by United for a Fair Economy, July 21, 2010.

104. "The Daphne Foundation," Daphne Foundation, http://www.daphnefoundation.org/history.htm (accessed October 29, 2011).

105. "Award Winners 2008," TribecaFilm.com, http://www.tribecafilm.com/home/18455719.html (accessed October 29, 2011).

106. "Award-Winning Filmmaker to Speak at UCR," University of California, Riverside, http://newsroom.ucr.edu/2618 (accessed October 29, 2011).

107. See note 12 above.

108. See note 103 above.

109. See note 12 above.

110. See note 103 above.

111. Chuck Collins interviewed Jim Sherblom on December 12, 2003, and March 23, 2010. Mike Lapham interviewed Sherblom on July 18, 2011. Unless otherwise specified, all subsequent information was obtained from those interviews.

Chapter 5: Policy Implications and the Public Investment Imperative

1. Dave Kellogg, "Rise Early, Work Hard, and Strike Oil," Kellblog, December 10, 2008, http://kellblog.com/2008/12/10/rise-early-work-hard-and-strike-oil (accessed October 28, 2011).

2. Garrison Keillor, "We're Not in Lake Wobegon Anymore," August 27, 2004, http://www.commondreams.org/views04/0831-02.htm (accessed October 28, 2011).

3. Mark Harrison, "The Seven Deadly Sins of Government-Funded Schools," *Chattanooga Times Free Press*, August 14, 2005, http://www.cato.org/pub _display.php?pub_id=4178 (accessed October 28, 2011).

4. Karlyn Bowman and Andrew Rugg, "New Lows and Highs: What You May Have Missed in the Polls," The American, August 5, 2011, http://blog.american .com/tag/congressional-approval (accessed October 29, 2011).

5. Mark Zandi, "The Economic Outlook and Stimulus Options," Moody's Analytics, http://www.economy.com/mark-zandi/documents/Senate_Budget _Committee_11_19_08.pdf (accessed October 29, 2011).

6. Adam Liptak, "Justices, 5-4, Reject Corporate Spending Limit," *New York Times*, January 21, 2010, http://www.nytimes.com/2010/01/22/us/politics/22scotus .html (accessed October 29, 2011).

7. Adam Smith, *The Wealth of Nations* (New York: Modern Library), 888.

8. "Adam Smith, the Adam Smith Institute, and Flat Taxes," The Tax Justice Network, January 4, 2010, http://taxjustice.blogspot.com/2010/01/adam -smith-adam-smith-institute-and.html (accessed October 29, 2011).

9. "Schakowsky Introduces Bill to Tax Millionaires and Billionaires," Congress-woman Jan Schakowsky, March 16, 2011, http://schakowsky.house.gov/ index.php?option=com_content&view=article&id=2877&catid=22 (accessed October 29, 2011).

10. Warren Buffett, "Stop Coddling the Super-Rich," *New York Times*, August 14, 2011, http://www.nytimes.com/2011/08/15/opinion/stop-coddling-the-super -rich.html (accessed October 28, 2011).

11. "State Individual Income Tax Rates, 2000–2011," Tax Foundation, March 3, 2011, http://www.taxfoundation.org/taxdata/show/228.html (accessed October 29, 2011).

12. "2011 Federal Income Tax Brackets and Marginal Rates," Consumerism Commentary, updated October 24, 2011, http://www.consumerismcommentary .com/federal-income-tax-brackets-and-marginal-rates (accessed October 29, 2011).

13. "Dividend Tax Rates: What Investors Need to Know," Investopedia, March 6, 2011, http://www.investopedia.com/articles/06/JGTRRADividends.asp#ixzz1 VDiR4lPa (accessed October 29, 2011).

14. "The People's Budget: Budget of the Congressional Progressive Caucus, Fiscal Year 2012," US House of Representatives, http://grijalva.house.gov/uploads/ The%20CPC%20FY2012%20Budget.pdf (accessed October 29, 2011).

15. "Proposals to Tax Wealth Like Work," United for a Fair Economy, April 7, 2001, http://www.faireconomy.org/enews/proposals_to_tax_wealth_like_work (accessed October 29, 2011).

16. Jackie Calmes, "Obama Tax Plan Would Ask More of Millionaires," *New York Times,* September 17, 2011, http://www.nytimes.com/2011/09/18/us/politics/ obama-tax-plan-would-ask-more-of-millionaires.html?pagewanted=all (accessed October 29, 2011).

17. Andrew Carnegie, *World's Work XVII* (New York: Doubleday, Page, 1909), 11050, as cited in Irvin G. Wyllie, *The Self-Made Man in America: The Myth of Rags to Riches* (New Brunswick: Rutgers University Press, 1954), 89–90.

18. "Estate Tax Speaker: Jerry Fiddler," United for a Fair Economy, http://faireconomy .org/issues/estate_tax/estate_tax_teleconference_november_2010/estate_tax _speaker_jerry_fiddler (accessed October 29, 2011).

19. Robert Rubin and Julian Robertson, "Bring Back the Estate Tax Now," *Wall Street Journal,* September 1, 2010, http://online.wsj.com/article/SB10001424 0527487039597045754540739828 25164.html (accessed October 29, 2011).

20. "Estate Tax Statement from John C. Bogle, Founder of the Vanguard Group," United for a Fair Economy, December 15, 2009, http://faireconomy.org/news/ estate_tax_statement_from_john_bogle (accessed October 29, 2011).

21. William H. Gates Sr. and Chuck Collins, *Wealth and Our Commonwealth: Why America Should Tax Accumulated Fortunes* (Boston: Beacon Press, 2002).

22. Kevin Drawbaugh, "Buffett Backs Estate Tax, Decries Wealth Gap," Reuters, November 14, 2007, http://www.reuters.com/article/2007/11/14/us-buffett -congress-idUSN1442383020071114 (accessed October 29, 2011).

23. Carmen DeNavas-Walt, Bernadette D. Proctor, and Jessica C. Smith, "Income, Poverty, and Health Insurance Coverage in the United States: 2009," US Census Bureau, September 2010, http://www.census.gov/prod/2010pubs/ p60-238.pdf (accessed October 29, 2011).

24. Administrator, "Sander [*sic*] Forwards Estate Tax Fix That Inflicts Pain on the Wealthy," *The Hill,* June 25, 2010, http://thehill.com/blogs/on-the-money/ domestic-taxes/105559-sander-forwards-estate-tax-fix-that-inflicts-pain-on -the-wealthy (accessed October 29, 2011).

25. Philip Rucker, "Mitt Romney Says 'Corporations Are People' at Iowa State Fair," *Washington Post,* August 11, 2011, http://www.washingtonpost.com/ politics/mitt-romney-says-corporations-are-people/2011/08/11/gIQABwZ38I _story.html (accessed October 29, 2011).

26. Catherine Poe, "Top Ten List: Tax Evaders' Wall of Shame," Washington Times Communities, April 11, 2011, http://communities.washingtontimes .com/neighborhood/ad-lib/2011/apr/10/tax-evaders-wall-shame (accessed October 29, 2011).

27. "G.E. and Corporate Tax Fairness," A Civil American Debate, March 29, 2011, http://acivilamericandebate.wordpress.com/2011/03/29/g-e-and-corporate -tax-fairness (accessed October 29, 2011).

28. Chuck Collins, "The Business Case against Overseas Tax Havens," *Huffington Post,* July 20, 2010, http://www.huffingtonpost.com/chuck-collins/the-business -case-against_b_652832.html (accessed October 29, 2011).

29. Stephen Lacey, "Obama Proposes Cutting Oil and Gas Subsidies $41 Billion to Help Fund Jobs Package," Think Progress, September 13, 2011, http:// thinkprogress.org/romm/2011/09/13/318266/fund-jobs-package-obama proposes cutting oil and gas subsidies (accessed September 30, 2011).

30. George Washington, State of the Union Address 1790, January 8, 1790, InfoPlease, http://www.infoplease.com/t/hist/state-of-the-union/1.html #ixzz1Q74LcPOs (accessed October 28, 2011).

31. See note 5 above.

32. "Estimated Impact of the American Recovery and Reinvestment Act on Employment and Economic Output from April 2011 through June 2011," Congressional Budget Office, August 2011, http://www.cbo.gov/ftpdocs/123xx/ doc12385/08-24-ARRA.pdf (accessed October 29, 2011).

33. "Summary: Opportunity in America," *The Future of Children* 16 (fall 2006), http://www.brookings.edu/es/research/projects/foc/foc_16_2_summary.pdf (accessed October 29, 2011).

34. Dean Baker, "Will Obamacare Make the US More Like Europe?" *Huffington Post,* August 4, 2009, http://www.huffingtonpost.com/dean-baker/will -obamacare-make-the-u_b_250768.html (accessed October 29, 2011).

35. Ibid.

36. Ha-Joon Chang, *23 Things They Don't Tell You about Capitalism* (New York: Bloomsbury Press, 2010), 3.

37. Mike Lapham interviewed Amy Domini on July 6, 2011.

38. Nick Carey, "Special Report: Is America the Sick Man of the Globe?" Reuters, December 16, 2010, http://www.reuters.com/article/2010/12/16/us-usa-economy-special-idUSTRE6BF28720101216 (accessed October 29, 2011).

39. "Estate Tax Speaker: Jean Gordon," United for a Fair Economy, http:// faireconomy.org/estate_tax_teleconference_nov_2010/jean_gordon (accessed October 28, 2011).

40. "About the King Arthur Flour Company," King Arthur Flour, http://www .kingarthurflour.com/about (accessed October 29, 2011).

41. "Frequently Asked Questions," New Belgium Brewing, http://www.new belgium.com/culture/faq.aspx (accessed October 29, 2011).

42. Sarah Anderson, Chuck Collins, Scott Klinger, and Sam Pizzigati, "Executive Excess 2011: The Massive CEO Rewards for Tax Dodging," Institute for Policy Studies, August 31, 2011, http://www.ips-dc.org/reports/executive _excess_2011_the_massive_ceo_rewards_for_tax_dodging/ (accessed October 29, 2011).

43. "Shareholder Votes on Executive Compensation at US Firms Have Been Judicious as well as Effective, New Research Finds," American Accounting Association, July 21, 2010, http://aaahq.org/newsroom/ShareholderVotes.htm (accessed October 29, 2011).

44. Labor Law Center, "Federal Minimum Wage Increase for 2007, 2008, and 2009," http://www.laborlawcenter.com/t-federal-minimum-wage.aspx (accessed October 29, 2011).

45. "Minimum Wage History," Oregon State University, updated February 22, 2011, http://oregonstate.edu/instruct/anth484/minwage.html (accessed October 29, 2011).

46. Todd J. Kumler, "Living Wage Ordinances," *Res Publica—Journal of Undergraduate Research* 12 (2007), http://digitalcommons.iwu.edu/respublica/vol12/ iss1/4 (accessed October 29, 2011).

47. Mazher Ali, Jeannette Huezo, Brian Miller, Wanjiku Mwangi, and Mike Prokosch, *State of the Dream 2011: Austerity for Whom?* (Boston: United for a Fair Economy, 2011), v.

48. Ibid.

Conclusion: A Call to Action

1. Transcript: Bill Moyers Interviews Bill Gates Sr. and Chuck Collins, PBS, January 17, 2003, http://www.pbs.org/now/transcript/transcript_inheritance.html (accessed October 29, 2011).

2. Ashlea Ebeling, "Tax Me, Please," *Forbes,* October 6, 2010, http://www.forbes.com/sites/ashleaebeling/2010/10/06/tax-me-please (accessed October 29, 2011).

3. Warren E. Buffett, "Stop Coddling the Super-Rich," *New York Times,* August 14, 2011, http://www.nytimes.com/2011/08/15/opinion/stop-coddling-the-super-rich.html?_r=1&hp (accessed October 29, 2011).

4. Jim Kuhnhenn, "Obama Unveils Deficit Reduction Plan, 'Buffett Rule' Tax on Millionaires," *Huffington Post,* September 19, 2011, http://www.huffingtonpost.com/2011/09/19/obama-deficit-plan-buffet-rule-taxes-medicare_n_969403.html (accessed October 29, 2011).

Acknowledgments

This book would not exist without the dozen successful entrepreneurs who took time out of their crowded schedules to be interviewed for the profiles in chapter 4. We are indebted to Nikhil Arora, Peter Barnes, Anirvan Chatterjee, Ben Cohen, Gun Denhart, Amy Domini, Jerry Fiddler, Kim Jordan, Thelma Kidd, Glynn Lloyd, Martin Rothenberg, and Jim Sherblom; to Abigail Disney for agreeing to be profiled; and to Warren Buffett for being a beacon of wisdom on fair taxation and calling things like he sees them.

Our thanks to our publishers for their thoughtful guidance and support, especially Steven Piersanti, who was so passionate about this book that he refused to delegate it to anyone else, and to the dedicated staff at Berrett-Koehler Publishers, all of whom have been remarkably kind and patient and helpful, and helpfully *im*patient, in bringing this project to fruition. Thanks as well to the production team at Ideas to Images for helping turn our words into the book you're looking at today.

For their invaluable assistance with research, transcription, writing, editing, and sharing their ideas, we warmly thank our terrific research assistants, in order of appearance: Sara Bodner, Jonathan Dame, Elisha Baskin, Maggie Hanley, and Danielle Bodnar. We also extend our gratitude to Will Rice, Mike Prokosch, and Tim Sullivan, who provided writing and editorial assistance at key points in this project.

And to our early reviewers, including Jeffrey Kullick, Richard Landry, Nicole Richards, Tamara Schweitzer, and Shaula Shames, this book is stronger because of your input.

This book has its roots in a 2004 report by the Responsible Wealth project at United for a Fair Economy titled "I Didn't Do It Alone: Society's Contribution to Individual Wealth and Success," which was co-authored by Chuck Collins, Mike Lapham, and Scott Klinger. That report provided the inspiration and the framework for this book. Parts of the 2004 report, including some of the profiles, were adapted and revised for use in this book. We are indebted to Chuck and Scott for their excellent work in the inception and development of the 2004 report.

We are grateful to our fellow staff members at United for a Fair Economy and the Responsible Wealth project, all of whom have contributed ideas and assistance to this endeavor in ways large and small. UFE has an extraordinarily creative, talented, and dedicated staff, and we are lucky to be working among them. Thanks as well to all of those whose financial support makes the work of United for a Fair Economy and Responsible Wealth possible, including the countless hours of research and writing that went into the production of this book.

Thanks also to the many who helped us brainstorm and bounce ideas around, participated in surveys, and offered their valuable advice, assistance, and feedback. There are too many of you to name, but you know who you are! Thank you.

Index

About the Authors

Brian Miller

Brian Miller is the executive director of United for a Fair Economy. Over the past 20 years, Miller has worked to build cross-class alliances of citizens from all walks of life—business leaders, workers, family farmers, seniors, students, and others—to work together for change, promoting healthy communities and an economy that works for all Americans.

A native of south Louisiana, Miller has a unique perspective on business and market economics. As the son of a stockbroker and an accountant, Miller was educated early about the workings of the stock market in a household surrounded by statues of bulls, bears, and ticker tape awards.

Miller received his degree in political science, with a secondary focus in economics from the University of Louisiana at Lafayette. Throughout both his academic and professional careers, Miller has sought to deepen his understanding of the points where public policy intersects with economics.

In addition to efforts in his home state of Louisiana, Miller has helped move campaigns and organizing efforts across the South and the Midwest. Some of his earliest experiences in Louisiana centered on the abuse of corporate tax breaks that left schools without adequate resources. He also helped grassroots leaders successfully

PHOTO BY DARIA GERE

protect their community from an unwanted hazardous waste facility south of Baton Rouge, and he helped farmers in Kentucky secure cost-sharing funds to pay for water-quality buffers.

Most of Miller's experience comes from his 12 years as executive director of Tennesseans for Fair Taxation (TFT). As director of TFT, he was an integral part of a historic fight that brought the state to within five votes of enacting a state income tax as part of a broader tax reform package to fund education and other services—an effort that was supported by business groups and community groups alike.

Miller took over as executive director of United for a Fair Economy in 2009. At UFE he has continued his commitment to cross-class organizing, working with grassroots groups, unions, and business leaders. He has also helped organize business leaders and other high-wealth individuals in support of progressive tax reform efforts. In this role he has worked with a wide array of business leaders, including some of those profiled in this book.

The author of numerous reports garnering coverage in major national publications such as the *New York Times* and the *Washington Post,* Miller has also appeared on national television programs like *Fox Business.* He is a frequent guest on radio programs and has been quoted in major media outlets across the nation. He is a regular op-ed writer and a contributor to various online and print publications.

Miller is an avid cyclist and an active member of his community. He lives in Waltham, Massachusetts, with his wife, Daria, and their two young children.

PHOTO BY CHRISTINE INKYUNG KIM

Mike Lapham

Mike Lapham is the founding director of Responsible Wealth, a project of United for a Fair Economy. Responsible Wealth amplifies the voices of more than 700 progressive business leaders and other affluent individuals in public policy debates to promote progressive tax policy and greater corporate accountability in Congress, in the media, and in corporate boardrooms.

Born in Glens Falls, New York, the youngest of four boys, Lapham was raised in Rochester, where he attended excellent and well-funded public schools. He earned his BA at Dartmouth College, where he majored in urban studies and public policy and wrote his honors thesis, "The History and Causes of Homelessness." He later received a master's degree in community economic development (the nonprofit equivalent of an MBA) from New Hampshire College.

Lapham was a fifth-generation owner of the Finch, Pruyn & Co. paper mill in Glens Falls, New York, co-founded by his great-great-grandfather Samuel Pruyn in 1865 and sold in 2007. Lapham donated more than half a million dollars of his income in the 1980s and 1990s to nonprofit organizations doing community organizing and social change work.

Lapham inherited a passion for economic and social justice from his parents, who were active in civil rights and economic justice efforts. Following college, he spent 10 years developing affordable housing in both the private and public sectors. As a housing specialist at Mintz Levin law firm in Boston, Lapham gained experience in the financial and legal aspects of housing development, becoming a statewide expert in use of the Comprehensive Permit Law to build mixed-income housing.

In 1990 Lapham joined the City of Boston's Public Facilities Department as a project manager, working with both for- and nonprofit developers, service providers, and neighborhood groups to create housing for people with AIDS, the homeless, and the mentally ill. He became the city's AIDS housing project manager, leading the campaign to develop 500 units of AIDS housing in Boston. His six years of working for the city provided insight on the importance of public programs as well as the challenge of working in the public sector, where expectations are high but resources are limited.

In 1997 Lapham co-founded and became the founding director of the Responsible Wealth project at United for a Fair Economy. Thanks to the support of his colleagues at UFE and the dedicated members of Responsible Wealth around the country, the project continues to thrive. Lapham is regularly interviewed for regional and national print publications and is a frequent guest commentator on CNBC, MSNBC, Fox, and various radio programs.

Lapham rides his bike to work year-round on public roads, bike paths, and bike lanes and is an avid squash player. He lives in Jamaica Plain, Massachusetts, with his wife, Amanda, and their three young children.

About Responsible Wealth

Responsible Wealth, a project of United for a Fair Economy, was founded in 1997 to give a voice to business leaders and wealthy individuals who believe that the economic rules of the US economy are tilted in their favor and that growing economic inequality is not in their long-term best interest.

Responsible Wealth's 700 members nationwide are individuals and couples in the top 5 percent of family income and/or wealth who are tired of being used as the poster children for regressive policies they don't support. They are business owners, investors, heirs, and others who advocate for more-progressive tax policies, responsible budgets, and greater corporate accountability. Responsible Wealth's members and staff write letters to the editor and op-eds, sign open letters, speak to the media, contact their elected officials, and use their stock ownership to file shareholder resolutions on executive compensation, corporate governance, political influence, and other topics.

In each of these cases, the "man bites dog" nature of affluent individuals' speaking out against their narrow financial self-interest in favor of the common good provides a powerful and much-needed counterbalance to the anti-tax, anti-government, free-market narrative that often fills the airwaves, dominates corporate boardrooms, and pervades the halls of Congress. The surprising voices of Responsible Wealth members have turned heads, elicited tears, and at times turned the tide of public debate on issues of taxation, wages, and corporate accountability.

One particularly clear example of Responsible Wealth's effectiveness has been on the estate tax. When George W. Bush made repeal of the estate tax his number one priority—the "engine" of his tax cut plans—Responsible Wealth quickly made it the caboose, taking out a *New York Times* ad, recruiting more than 2,000 wealthy signers of its Call to Preserve the Estate Tax, organizing lobby days, and speaking to the media about why the country needs a strong estate tax. Though weakened, the estate tax has not been repealed in the years since, despite many attempts, in large part thanks to wealthy proponents of the tax, including the members of Responsible Wealth.

Another strong example of Responsible Wealth's impact came in 2009, when the state of New York faced a $19 billion budget shortfall. Responsible Wealth (with its state partner, New Yorkers for Fiscal Fairness) organized more than 90 upper-income New Yorkers to sign an open letter to the governor and the legislature, saying, in effect, "tax us" to help fill the gap. Although everyone knew that this was what needed to be done, nobody was willing to say it publicly—not the politicians, not the media—until after Responsible Wealth's letter was delivered. Soon thereafter the state enacted a tax surcharge on incomes over $200,000, with a second tier starting at $500,000, that accounted for more than $4 billion in new annual revenue.

As the nation (and the states) continue to debate policies around taxes, budgets, the role of government, and corporate accountability, Responsible Wealth will continue to play an important role in turning heads and influencing public policy. For more information contact Responsible Wealth at info@responsible wealth.org or call (617) 423-2148.

About United for a Fair Economy

United for a Fair Economy is a national, nonprofit organization founded in 1995 to raise awareness that concentrated wealth and power undermines the economy, corrupts democracy, deepens the racial wealth divide, and tears communities apart. In working to achieve a more broadly shared prosperity, UFE works to shape public dialogue, support grassroots movements, and directly effect policy change.

The heart of UFE's work is its popular education workshops, which have been attended by tens of thousands of individuals, including its flagship workshop, The Growing Divide and the Roots of Economic Insecurity. UFE's popular education methodology draws on participants' own values and experiences of the economy. UFE works with partner organizations across the United States to train grassroots leaders to use this methodology to engage communities on issues of inequality.

UFE's Racial Wealth Divide project explores the historical and contemporary barriers to wealth creation for people of color. From this work grows UFE's *State of the Dream* report, released each year in conjunction with Martin Luther King Jr. Day. These reports bring national attention to pressing issues like predatory subprime lending and the disproportionate impact of the Great Recession on communities of color.

United for a Fair Economy supports progressive taxation at both the federal and state levels. Since 2000 UFE has been a leading advocate in the successful effort to preserve a strong estate tax, working with a number of national coalitions and state-level partners. UFE has also pushed for more-progressive federal income taxes, stronger corporate taxes, and ending special tax breaks for investment income, as an alternative to harmful budget cuts. UFE's work on this front has been widely covered in the national media.

In 2004 UFE created the Tax Fairness Organizing Collaborative to act as the national network of groups organizing for progressive taxation at the state level. Since its founding, the TFOC has grown, with member groups now working in 24 states across the country. UFE provides training and support to the TFOC member organizations, organizes affinity groups around specific challenges (like states without an income tax), and brings the state groups together at national gatherings to share strategies.

UFE's Responsible Wealth project organizes upper-income and wealthy individuals to use their voices to promote progressive taxation and corporate accountability. Through Responsible Wealth, UFE has built powerful cross-class alliances that have helped energize and strengthen their shared work toward a more fair economy (see "About Responsible Wealth" for more information).

Finally, UFE uses its communications capacity to provide a wealth of information and resources about economic inequality and the policy choices of our day. Interactive tools, videos, infographics, and more are available on UFE's website at www .faireconomy.org.

Together UFE's unique mix of movement support, popular education, media work, tax organizing, and mobilizing upper-income business leaders and investors make the organization an important part of the economic justice movement. For more information contact United for a Fair Economy at info@faireconomy .org, visit www.faireconomy.org, or call (617) 423-2148.

Berrett–Koehler
Publishers

Berrett-Koehler is an independent publisher dedicated to an ambitious mission: *Creating a World That Works for All.*

We believe that to truly create a better world, action is needed at all levels—individual, organizational, and societal. At the individual level, our publications help people align their lives with their values and with their aspirations for a better world. At the organizational level, our publications promote progressive leadership and management practices, socially responsible approaches to business, and humane and effective organizations. At the societal level, our publications advance social and economic justice, shared prosperity, sustainability, and new solutions to national and global issues.

A major theme of our publications is "Opening Up New Space." Berrett-Koehler titles challenge conventional thinking, introduce new ideas, and foster positive change. Their common quest is changing the underlying beliefs, mindsets, institutions, and structures that keep generating the same cycles of problems, no matter who our leaders are or what improvement programs we adopt.

We strive to practice what we preach—to operate our publishing company in line with the ideas in our books. At the core of our approach is stewardship, which we define as a deep sense of responsibility to administer the company for the benefit of all of our "stakeholder" groups: authors, customers, employees, investors, service providers, and the communities and environment around us.

We are grateful to the thousands of readers, authors, and other friends of the company who consider themselves to be part of the "BK Community." We hope that you, too, will join us in our mission.

A BK Currents Book

This book is part of our BK Currents series. BK Currents books advance social and economic justice by exploring the critical intersections between business and society. Offering a unique combination of thoughtful analysis and progressive alternatives, BK Currents books promote positive change at the national and global levels. To find out more, visit **www.bkconnection.com**.

Berrett–Koehler
Publishers
A community dedicated to creating
a world that works for all

Visit Our Website: www.bkconnection.com

Read book excerpts, see author videos and Internet movies, read
our authors' blogs, join discussion groups, download book apps, find
out about the BK Affiliate Network, browse subject-area libraries of
books, get special discounts, and more!

Subscribe to Our Free E-Newsletter, the *BK Communiqué*

Be the first to hear about new publications, special discount offers,
exclusive articles, news about bestsellers, and more! Get on the list
for our free e-newsletter by going to **www.bkconnection.com**.

Get Quantity Discounts

Berrett-Koehler books are available at quantity discounts for orders
of ten or more copies. Please call us toll-free at (800) 929-2929 or
email us at bkp.orders@aidcvt.com.

Join the BK Community

BKcommunity.com is a virtual meeting place where people from
around the world can engage with kindred spirits to create a world
that works for all. BKcommunity.com members may create their own
profiles, blog, start and participate in forums and discussion groups,
post photos and videos, answer surveys, announce and register for
upcoming events, and chat with others online in real time. Please join
the conversation!